D1511788

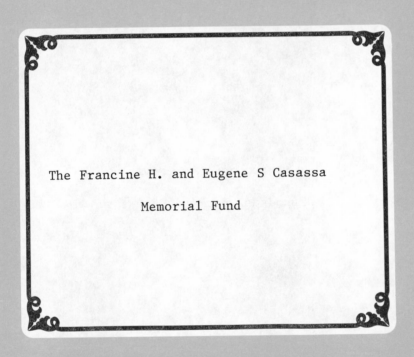

The Francine H. and Eugene S Casassa

Memorial Fund

I'M A BORN LIAR I'M A BORN LIAR
BORN LIAR I'M A BORN LIAR I'M
BORN LIAR I'M A BORN LIAR I'M
LIAR I'M A BORN LIAR I'M A BORN LIA
BORN LIAR I'M A BORN LIAR I'M A BOR
I'M A BORN LIAR I'M A BORN LIA
BORN LIAR I'M A BORN LIAR I'M
BORN LIAR I'M A BORN LIAR I'M
LIAR I'M A BORN LIAR I'M A BORN
I'M A BORN LIAR I'M A BORN L
A BORN LIAR I'M A BORN LIAR I'M A B

edited by **DAMIAN** PETTIGREW I'M A BORN LI

A BORN LIAR I'M A BORN LIAR I'M
BORN LIAR I'M A BORN LIAR I'M A B
I'M A BORN LIAR I'M A BORN LIAR I'
BORN LIAR I'M A BORN LIAR I'M A BO
LIAR I'M A BORN LIAR I'M A BOR
LIAR I'M A BORN LIAR I'M A BORN LIA
A BORN LIAR I'M A BORN LIAR I'M A
BORN LIAR I'M A BORN LIAR I'M A
LIAR I'M A BORN LIAR I'M A BORN

I'M A BORN LIAR *a fellini lexicon*

Harry N. Abrams, Inc., Publishers

6 *Introduction* Damian Pettigrew   8 *Truth & Poetry in Lies* Tullio Kezich

CONTENTS

12 *Lexicon: A to Z*   168 *Filmography*   176 *Photograph Credits*

Introduction

The idea of a series of long filmed interviews with Federico Fellini
first came to me in the summer of 1983 while producing and directing
a portrait of Italo Calvino for Canadian television. Since Calvino knew
Fellini well, having written the brilliant preface, "Autobiografia di uno
spettatore," for the director's *Quattro Film*, it was inevitable that we
discuss the great director's work. In fact, Fellini became our favorite
topic of discussion: Calvino was highly reluctant to reveal himself in
such an open forum as the filmed interview and constantly avoided
personal questions. He did, however, encourage me in my ambition to
explore the still nascent medium of interviewing artists on film,
advising me with wise and gentle words to focus on the artist's work
that results from the lies he tells about his life: it is those lies, those
"supreme fictions," that reveal what is most valuable about himself.
And so I have an enormous debt toward Calvino, for it was due to his
influence that I finally came into *Il Maestro*'s favor. ¶ The interviews
were recorded during two eight-hour taping sessions using three
Betacam SP cameras in the summers of 1991 and 1992. The production, independently financed, was to serve as the basis of a filmed
portrait of the artist and a book. I had prepared a list of two hundred
questions. Federico and I agreed that the first filmed sessions would
focus exclusively on his creative process and working methods. The
second filmed sessions would deal with the problem of grace, the
enigma of inspiration, and a few one-liners. ¶ The single greatest
influence on my work as a filmmaker has been the celebrated
Interviews with Francis Bacon (1980) by David Sylvester. Sylvester is a
master of the art of complicity: he knows exactly how to manipulate
and exploit complicity. Complicity requires being cautiously intel-

lectual yet profoundly human in the sense that the interviewer must act as the concerned midwife, allowing the interviewee to express himself while at the same time guiding his thoughts to a satisfactory conclusion through sensitive provocation. The psychological process is akin to a series of concentric circles where familiarity and formal respect are constantly being contracted to achieve the necessary *distance* that permits the interviewee to confess his innermost thoughts. In the case of a film director like Fellini, who was interviewed countless times, I felt it was absolutely necessary to provoke his anti-intellectualism in order to arrive at responses that weren't simply the recycled ideas he was fond of giving to the press. I didn't always succeed: the filmed interview is an art extemporized under difficult conditions and successful only when the interviewee hasn't prepared his replies beforehand. Urging Fellini—who was a genuinely mysterious, intensely private man—to carefully analyze his complex creative processes by criticizing his need to hide behind a digressive wall of words, in short, to have him isolate his aesthetic and moral world, was at once a daunting and exhilarating challenge. ¶ These recorded interviews are the texts published here and, like David Sylvester with Francis Bacon, I have bowed to their authority in handling Fellini's words. I have modified his texts only where he repeats himself or to clarify syntax, altering a word to improve clarity but never his speech rhythms or his unique roll of adjectives. In the effort to make these texts more readable, I have effaced almost all of my two hundred questions. In a way, they are Federico's "supreme fictions" inspired by memory and art, truth and contradiction.

DAMIAN PETTIGREW, May 2, 2003, Paris

Truth & Poetry in Lies

I confess that I like everything about this book, except for its title. By declaring, "I'm a born liar," Fellini risks endorsing a common perception that has hounded him for decades; it is crucial, then, that we differentiate a lie from a lie. It occurred to me that, having known both well, we could distinguish Fellini from his supposed maestro Rossellini in this way and in spite of their reputations as the patent liars of Roman cinema. Whereas Roberto's lie was functional, used to sort out urgent problems of life and work, Federico's was similar to the surreal utterance of the child who returns home from school and tells his mother, "On the road I met an elephant." One has to keep in mind the special felliniesque meaning of the word "lie." For Federico, wandering from the verifiable truth was to assert his creative right in the immediate arousal of fantasy, a magic ritual with which to enter the world of art. ¶ This does not mean that the author of *8 ½*, badgered by novices of every kind, never used Rossellini's "cover lie." He tried to fool those who telephoned (insatiably curious, he always answered the call himself) by imitating the housekeeper's voice: "I'm sorry, the Maestro is not in." Other times I heard him reply without travesty, using a more explicit though still elusive tactic: "We'll talk on Monday." It goes without saying that the Monday in question never arrived. Consequently, and in line with what Damian Pettigrew wrote me in a sympathetic letter, it comes as no surprise that even the initiator of these "marathon conversations" had to concoct various strategies to circumvent the felliniesque roadblock. Until 1983, already twenty years ago, when Italo Calvino opened the coveted door of the *sancta sanctorum* by inviting Damian to a private lunch at the Maestro's *pied-à-terre* at Cinecittà. ¶ Federico was going through a period in which, due to insomnia, he had transformed himself from the occasional consumer of books into an omnivorous and hyper-informed reader, capable of waking a writer at dawn if he had devoured his novel during the late night hours. Among the titles Fellini highly recommended was Calvino's *Italian Folktales*, a classic he wanted to adapt as a film. Their narrow circle of professional and artistic acquaintances was surprisingly accessible once the right point of entry was found and friends of friends were instantly adopted as new friends; indeed, the same thing happened to me fifty years ago when, through my friendship with Leopoldo Trieste, I became close to Fellini. The formal *you* was dropped and in a flood of familiarity, neophytes were given affectionate and diminutive nicknames that sounded like characters from a comic strip. I saw Anita Ekberg become Anitona; Anouk Aimée, Anucchina; Terence Stamp, Terenzino Francobollo; Donald Sutherland, Donaldino. I would be willing to gamble that Damian Pettigrew became something

Je suis un menteur qui dit toujours la vérité. JEAN COCTEAU

like Damianino Pettirosso. ¶ Towards the end of their lunch, having pleasantly meandered through such topics as French cheeses, neorealist landscapes, and elements of the absurd in Rossellini, the Canadian guest ventured the proposal that they expand their chat into an interview in front of the camera. On the spur of the moment, Fellini no doubt relegated the request to an improbable Monday, but the project took form soon afterwards in the shape and seriousness of a contract. In fact, someone had suggested to Damian that Fellini, having developed the habit as a screenwriter in search of funding, would easily sign a scrap of paper if it were baited with a solid advance. Nevertheless, more time passed until the start of principal photography on *The Voice of the Moon* when the Maestro called Pettigrew in person, proposing he draft an outline for an interview about his new film. ¶ At this moment, the Canadian made a masterful move: he declined. Unwilling to settle for one of the usual promotional statements, he preferred waiting out the opportunity to conduct an extended, more profound conversation. In any relationship with Fellini, playing coy was always a winning tactic. I heard Marcello Mastroianni jokingly theorize, "With Federico, you should never be too present or too available. It's wiser to make him jealous by playing hard-to-get. Just relax and know that sooner or later he'll come looking for you." It happened exactly like that in 1991, nine years after the unforgettable lunch with Calvino: once again, stubborn Damian was telephoned in Toronto and invited to come to Rome. The casual meeting they had arranged quickly developed into much more in the course of a pilgrimage they made together to Ostia, Fregene, Passo Oscuro, and other locations in the Fellini filmography. Pettigrew writes: "Federico was as talkative as ever but depressed and even bitter at times, often on the defensive, as if he felt the critics and his public had passed him over as too old and too repetitive." ¶ Let us pull back a moment to better appreciate the atmosphere in which the long interviews were filmed between 1991 and 1992, and examine the situation Fellini was in at the time. Since completing *The Voice of the Moon* in July 1989, the director had not set foot on a soundstage in over three years. The film had garnered favorable reviews without eliciting any enthusiasm. Wavering negotiations with public television for the special, *Actors*, dragged on relentlessly. While Fellini denounced the lethargic bureaucracy of state television, RAI executives blamed delays on his own procrastination. The upshot was that similar projects such as *Venice*, *Naples*, and *Dante's Inferno* were consigned *sine die* and left drifting aimlessly offshore. His health continued to deteriorate: he was plagued with circulatory problems and alarming bouts of dizziness. For his friends, however, the worst part was seeing how

Federico, little by little, adapted to his new life as an illustrious pensioner displaying a kind of feigned serenity. In a sudden rekindling of passion for his profession, he would return to his place behind the camera for a few days in June 1992 and, determined and focused, shoot three television commercials for the Banco di Roma with Paolo Villaggio. To his credit, Fellini refused a lucrative offer to play the part of the psychoanalyst, casting instead Spanish actor Fernando Rey in the lead role. ¶ Had he gone on to become a journalist, Federico would have been an incredible interviewer. He revealed himself to be a great interviewee, the best of them all. Any journalist who approached Fellini with a notebook, tape recorder, or video camera will attest that Fellini "wrote the article himself." Prompt to intuit the psychology of the interlocutor, his interests and his weak spots, he immediately anticipated the direction of the conversation, giving it a meaning, a tone, and a surprising liveliness. For the interviewer, there was little to do other than transcribe the director's words; occasionally, he repeated himself (granting hundreds of interviews in a single lifetime, he obviously ran the risk) but inevitably made up for it by adding some personal touch, a comment with a dash of the real or imaginary scoop so that the outcome was always professional. Culling material from past interviews (above all, I think, from those involving his congenial television accomplice Vincenzo Mollica), he would throw in a joke or a punch line here, a recollection there, perhaps a portrait skimmed off the top of his head, later a dazzling critique of a book or a film, or an unexpected commentary on news of the day. Fellini created the illusion of originality, the thrill of an exclusive. When in the mood, he undeniably carried himself with the air of the great self-promoter. But what I said earlier about Fellini's so-called lies also comes into play here: the apparent purpose of the interview, almost always the release of a new film, disappeared or was dissembled behind his genuine amusement in the situation, the pleasure of continuously re-inventing one of his own characters, the role play that slyly allowed him to usurp the interviewer's part—in short, to do exactly what he dreamed of doing ever since he was a child in Rimini: to play the journalist. And we note that he never tired of including journalists in his films: the bullshit artist in *A Marriage Agency*; the gossip columnists firing asinine questions at Anitona in *La Dolce Vita*; the stoic witness of the shipwreck in *And the Ship Sails On*. ¶ The survivor of this latter film resembles the defendant of *I'm a Born Liar*. The twilight tone of the images in *And the Ship Sails On*, where Federico appears stricken in years and at times decrepit, is translated onto the page. In the spotlight is no longer the master journalist but rather a sort of pensive philosopher. It is clear that Fellini is still himself: the matador of words, quick to strike with a witticism and drive home the right effect at the right time. On the other hand, his customary good cheer has now ceded to sudden waves of seriousness. Federico seems immersed in a moment in which it is no longer appropriate to trivialize things or slip into word games. The topics he touches on or delves into in these conversations have the weight of the largest existential questions drawn from an incredibly rich experience certain of its accomplishments and the stoic acceptance that, as the poet Umberto Saba expressed in his old age, "We know very little." For too many years, Fellini had constantly used irony to mock his attempts to probe the Great Mysteries, but judging from the way he responds to Pettigrew's questions, it seems he feels as though he were on the brink of a revelation. If the term "spiritual testament" could be used in reference to a personality like Fellini's, this interview-book would be it. And also because the fortunes of fate ordained that it should be the last time one of the major artists of the century was persuaded to talk about himself. ¶ I often wonder if Federico knew, as he seemed to at times during the last months of his life, that he was going to die and in some way began putting his house in order. The last afternoon that he was consciously present, on leave from the hospital, he went to visit the small artist's studio he had had renovated on the via Capo Le Case for the time when he was ready to return to a normal existence. True to his creative disposition, he was not perturbed by his own oblivion or by death as he prepared to exit the scene; instead, he planned his entrance into a new dimension of peaceful productivity. To be a painter was another childhood dream, on a level with journalism, and perhaps the moment had come in his life to ask, "Why not?" This movement of faith stirred from the depths a few traces of the religious education he had received as a child, later on neglected or contradicted by other demands, foolish aspirations, curiosity, and various skepticisms. It is not a coincidence that the title of the masterpiece he never directed, refusing the suggestion to have it re-christened *La Dolce Morte* as Dino Buzatti would have wished, remained *The Voyage of G. Mastorna*. Beyond the tangible, perhaps Fellini (I hope for his sake and it seems to me the confirmation can be found between the lines of this moving interview) managed to believe he was not at the end but at the beginning of something that was more than simply painting; something that in our poor existence as human beings we are prevented forever from imagining.

TULLIO KEZICH, May 7, 2003, Rome

Sylvia (Anita Ekberg) steps into the Trevi Fountain while Fellini (in hat, right) and Rome's male population closely monitor the scene. (*La Dolce Vita*, 1959)

LEFT: A *maestro* in the making: Fellini at the age of one. RIGHT: Rimini, September 1931: eleven-year-old Fellini (standing) with his younger brother, Riccardo.

THE ACTOR'S FACE

Growing up in Rimini, my brother Riccardo and I loved staging puppet shows. My first puppets were the Devil and Rausaria. We'd spend hours designing the costumes and the sets were spectacular. A lot less interesting, however, was the play itself: according to Mom and Dad, it was impossible to follow the plot. Patiently, I explained to them that the plot was incarnated in the grotesque faces of my puppets. For me, prewar cinema was always represented by an actor's face. For example, Garbo's sublime Pythia-like face magnified a hundred times on the big screen, or Chaplin's chalky mask, were faces that incarnated extremes of desire and psychological complexity. ¶ Nothing seems to have changed since those endless childhood days. Today, the critics complain that they don't understand the plots in my films, and I always reply that they don't know how to read faces. The way I make films frightens producers because I never offer them a script to read: I simply walk into their office, hand them some photos of an actor, and tell them a story while they puff away on smelly Cuban cigars. Either they go for it or they don't. The best producers I've worked with are excellent listeners: they sit back in their sumptuous leather chairs, usually with their feet on the desk, hands neatly folded in their laps—and they just listen, never interrupting, never yawning, never instructing their secretaries to bring them coffee, never taking calls. ¶ This may come as a shock but I directed *The Voice of the Moon* by writing each day's sequence the night before on a piece of paper. Once, while we were rehearsing, Roberto [Benigni] couldn't get the exact feel of a scene, no matter how many times I explained it to him. After the tenth take, I took out some felt pens and dotted my right palm in a splash of color. "That's the tone I'm after," I said. Roberto looked at his hand and

Twenty-year-old Fellini (left) with his brother, Riccardo (right), and a friend in Rome during the Christmas holidays, 1940.

understood instantly. You see, I don't think in terms of dialogue and plot twists: I think almost exclusively in images, which explains why an actor's face and body are more important to me than plot structure. When the scene has been constructed and works dramatically, words no longer have any importance. The only thing that has any true significance for me is living the moment on camera. ¶ The key word to understanding my kind of cinema is *vitality*. What I seek is to live the expression itself. The creature we call a movie is born by ignoring what you've spent months preparing to film, and if you can get the oxygen circulating, nothing else is necessary. The first two weeks, I direct the film; after that, the film directs me. I believe in that profoundly, despite the limits imposed by this working method and of which I am aware.

ACTS OF WILL

I was six years old, the story goes, when I first walked into a circus tent. I felt like Ulysses returning to Ithaca: I felt more at home in a circus than I had anywhere else. I'm not really sure why that was so, but it had to do with the aerial dimension of the circus, with the canvas that swells like a balloon, the deserted perspective, the red velvet chairs, the charged atmosphere, the horses, an invisible clown blowing a trumpet: all of it profoundly affected me. ¶ And then, as an adolescent, I discovered American films where the journalist was always more courageous than the entire police force and who, at the end, got to marry the blond actress. This convinced me for a time that I was a born journalist with a nose for a story and a head sculpted for hats like Bogey or Cagney wore. But soon, I realized that I wasn't gifted for squashing grapefruits in a lady's face. I thought to myself: I can't paint, I can't sculpt, I can't investigate. All I can do is

Titta (Bruno Zanin) discovers female sexuality in the arms of a tobacconist (Maria Beluzzi). (*Amarcord*, 1973)

draw ridiculous faces and fat female behinds. ¶ *Do you think that your decision to settle in Rome in 1939 was the decisive moment when you discovered that an artistic career was your future?* ¶ Well, I could tell you so many different versions of what happened that I no longer remember which one is the most charming of all the hundreds I've made up. But, for once, this shameless liar would like to be absolutely sincere. I do not recognize any particular acts of will on my part that can be described as personal ambition. I have never made a conscious decision that was influenced by the wish to obtain something career-wise. I've been extremely lucky in that respect: situations have always presented themselves to me in a spontaneous, generous way and I simply took them up, naturally and with gratitude, as if all of it were somehow predestined. My unique act of will was in not going against a particular situation but of acting on it, like Theseus with his thread. Of course, it's obvious that I've made key decisions in my life as a filmmaker and this is the most curious contradiction of all—to find a man like me making a thousand decisions a day in the course of a production: choosing the hunchback over the hook-nosed juggler and for the elephant—a handful of peanuts or six lumps of sugar? The striped pair of pantaloons or the bejeweled jacket and spiked boots? Plucked eyebrows and shorn lashes or a shaved head with a red wart? This snippet of dialogue with that tone of voice punctuated by a long pause or a short one or an abrupt silence altogether? And on and on. It's a profession where you are constantly called upon to make choices in record time and I hate having to choose: I always feel I'm losing something essential in the process and that, sooner or later, I'll have to compensate for it. There are times when having to choose leads to a state of paralysis. It's not surprising that Hamlet littered the stage with corpses. All of this to expose the role that decision-making

Fellini rehearsing with Franca Marzi who plays Wanda, Cabiria's best friend. (*The Nights of Cabiria*, 1957)

has in my life in pictures. For life in general, however, I have never decided or chosen anything that was crucial to pushing my career forward. I never sought out Rossellini for *Rome, Open City*; he came to me for help in scripting the story and I am eternally grateful. Rossellini walked into my life at a moment when I needed to make a choice, when I needed someone to show me the path to follow. He was the stationmaster, the green light of providence. I say that with enormous affection and in no way to diminish him. He was a friend, a mentor, a fabulous seducer who presented the filmmaker's way of life to me and, above all, the guide to how one achieves the quality of images nearest to one's own vision. Until then, I had been writing scripts for various directors, a job devoid of responsibility: scripts were something you wrote out at home in the kitchen over coffee. I never thought of becoming a director because I lacked the authority, the tyrant's awe-inspiring voice. I remember working in the theater and watching an actress botch her lines over and over again, blaming her incompetence on the hack writer and the hack writer throwing his manuscript in her face—in my view, a lot more unpleasant than a grapefruit! Once the stage director asked me to rewrite a scene and I found I couldn't focus my ideas, so disturbed was I by the total chaos around me, overwhelmed by the brash and aggressive atmosphere. I thought I could never prove my authority, order an actor to weep like a tragedian or giggle like a clown, impose an absolute silence or raise my voice and intimidate or master the art of direction in which the ends, it is hotly debated, justify the means. With my temperament, it seemed impossible for me not to fall in love with an actress. I saw beautiful actresses grossly insulted. I watched helpless as they broke down in tears and I thought that this violence, this use of force, was incompatible with my nature. All this, Rossellini effaced. Rossellini taught me how to thrive on

ABOVE: Showgirl Liliana Antonelli (Carla Del Poggio, right) performing in a vaudeville sketch inspired by the kind Fellini frequented at the Jovinelli variety theater in Rome. (*Variety Lights*, 1950) OPPOSITE: Fellini's first feature codirected with Alberto Lattuada: vagabond troupe leader Checco Dalmonte (Peppino De Filippo) shows off his eccentric performers to starlet Liliana Antonelli (Carla Del Poggio). (*Variety Lights*, 1950)

chaos by ignoring it and focusing on what was essential: constructing your film day by day. He taught me the tranquility of mind that a monk has, taking the film set as your monastery. I learned that one could make films with the same simplicity, care, and attention with which a writer pent up in his room could write a novel or that a painter in his atelier, as I saw as a child, could take a canvas, set it on his easel and without the least idea of what he was going to paint, begin painting a work that little by little became a full-fledged work of art. ¶ It is a fact that my career as a director was instigated by my colleague Alberto Lattuada, who suggested I codirect *Variety Lights*. I never asked for the honor. The same applies to the films I've directed. Once the possibility of two projects presented themselves to me, I chose the one I felt most comfortable with while deeply regretting, indeed resenting, the sacrifice involved. It is as if I were a train and my films the various stations that the train runs through in a familiar, predetermined itinerary. And so I found the films I needed to make waiting for me. I had to go on to direct them, of course, but their walls were already standing, their platforms swept clean, the rails laid end to end. In 1953, I pulled into the station of *I Vitelloni*; in 1969, *Satyricon*; in 1990, *The Voice of the Moon*. I honestly cannot recall having scripted with minute precision any film I ever made because each ripened inside me and was plucked or dropped, shipped for production, and, to a certain degree, already directed. The film simply required being directed in a concrete way. ¶ I'm aware that my conception of filmmaking is highly unorthodox and that's why I frighten producers. Here again, I don't go wandering off on my nag, Quixote-like, searching for producers in windmill shapes. No, usually they come to me, telling me what a Fellini film is and how I ought to entice my public.

19

Village beauty and object of masculine desire, La Gradisca ("If you please") played by Magali Noël, with girlfriends on parade. (*Amarcord*, 1973)

ADDICTION

I was a chain smoker up until I came down with Sanarelli-Schwarzmann Syndrome during production of
The Voyage of G. Mastorna in 1967. It's a profoundly debilitating allergy that affects one in ten million people
and so, naturally, I was very proud to have been selected among the happy few. Anyone who's had his heart
and lungs in the grip of an unpronounceable disease has no trouble kicking a measly nicotine addiction.

AMARCORD

I have often simplified the cabalistic meanings of the word *amarcord* by saying that it was *romagnol* [dialect
of the Emilia-Romagna region] for "I remember." But that's not quite true. I think the original idea came
to me after reading about a Swedish abortionist named Hammercord, the sound of which simply started
the ball rolling. If you contract *amare* (to love), *core* (heart), *ricordare* (to remember), and *amaro* (bitter),
you end up with *Amar-cor-d*.

AMERICA

I don't think an Italian of my generation, even the most hardened communist of my age group, could say
anything bad about America because, indubitably, even those who angrily contested capitalism and the
ideologies of the American way of life know they acted in bad faith. During the thirties and forties,
America narrated, in the most extraordinary way, fairytales for adults that enabled us to survive the paralysis and suffocation, the neurosis, the nightmare that was life under a Fascist dictatorship. If America

Even when drunk and in drag, Alberto (Alberto Sordi) is the most lucid of all the vitelloni. (*I Vitelloni*, 1953)

hadn't existed, I would have ended up a *vitelloni*. It's because America invented the movies—and thus a genuine popular culture that belongs to everyone—and because during my youth in Rimini, between school, family, Church, and Fascism, America represented another reality, one that replaced the boredom, the sadness of provincial life, the grayness, the eternal winter seasons, the fog that made it all the more intolerable to have to go to school; and then the military parades, the Fascist Saturdays, holy mass, confession, all the rituals of a little province closed in on this oppressive and suffocating ideology. It was possible to live through all that precisely because America sent us films that showed us another way of life, another country, a place where things were experienced with a joyous sense of adventure, with really beautiful women, and sympathetic leading men who were like Homeric heroes—Achilles and Hector. Through its films, America projected a self-portrait, a testimony that was so joyful, so vital, and one that we were more than willing to accept—for my generation at least—and be grateful for. At that time, America represented for Italy the dream of a new life, the alternative to a life of guns and military marches. So if I chose to make films it's really thanks to America. ¶ *You evoke American cinema and popular culture as major influences but comic strips also are a part of our culture.* ¶ Yes, there's an umbilical cord that links me to this country for which I'm forever grateful. The first news I ever had of America came in the form of comic strips from the golden age of the 1930s, classics like *Felix the Cat*, the *Happy Hooligan*, *Maggi and Jiggs*, *Popeye*, and the *Katzenjammer Kids*. I even tried, much later, in films like *Satyricon* and *The Clowns*, to recapture the characteristic colors of the comic strips of my youth. I'm talking about a country that expressed itself in a smile, with a sense of humor, at a time when here in Italy everything was deadly

Fellini on the Cinema Fulgor set showing Bruno Zanin (Titta) how to place his hand on Magali Noël's knee (La Gradisca). (*Amarcord*, 1973)

Sylvia (Anita Ekberg), the embodiment of an innocent and vital sensuality. (*La Dolce Vita*, 1959)

serious, nothing but sacrifice and mortification—mortification of the flesh—that delirious ecstasy of all things Roman. As I say, America was the providential fable that helped us to endure the bleakness of a totally artificial life disguised and betrayed by twin ideologies that went against life: Catholicism, which considered life a misery to be endured and the flesh an abomination, and Fascism, which ordered you to die for your country. Thank God there was Fred Astaire, Mae West, the Marx Brothers, and Mickey Mouse.

ANITA EKBERG

Anita Ekberg was a glorious apparition! I thought to myself, well, well, these are her ears, her eyes, her hair, and these.... She was like phosphorus, an extraterrestrial with a lunar pallor in her face and hair. It's been a long time since I last saw Anita. Watching her weather so many seasons as she has ... I particularly appreciate her because in one of my films, a *filmetto* called *Intervista*, I narrated a visit with Mastroianni to her villa in the country. She's a woman of a certain age who's put on weight, who lives with her dogs and ducks, like a happy peasant. And I saw she'd aged gracefully, a tranquil aging, sober, wise.... She's no longer the glorious diva, the Olympian she once was but she seems to me a beautiful example of serenity. ¶ *Of resignation?* ¶ Of acceptance.

ANOUK AIMÉE

I often described Anouk Aimée as a little girl with a metaphysical sensuality, unbelievably timid one moment and a man-eating shark the next. I didn't mean it to be an unkind image but a confirmation of her

A highly focused Fellini surveys the man-eating Maddalena (Anouk Aimée). (*La Dolce Vita*, 1959)

talent to beguile, a quality necessary for my Maddalena in *La Dolce Vita*. The narrative mechanism of that film focused on the identification of the enemy to be expelled, as in the detective story, and Anoukine was instrumental in depicting an ambiguous creature that was neither friend nor foe: "Are you," Marcello keeps asking her, "what you profess to be?" She's like a princess wearing the Crown of the Controller of Desires.

ARTISTIC CRISIS

Between La Dolce Vita *and* 8½, *there's a period of relative inactivity. Were you going through a spiritual or artistic crisis?* ¶ An artistic crisis. What self-respecting artist can do without one? ¶ *And this artistic crisis became the inspiration for* 8½? ¶ Yes. The idea behind it was very ambitious—I wanted to describe in a film how our everyday lives are multidimensional, where past, present, and future intermingle constantly—so much so that I couldn't express it. The idea was to deal with the protagonist's inner life in such a way that consciousness and the unconscious unfold like smoke rings. After *La Dolce Vita*, I felt a malaise that I was incapable of understanding. It was certainly existential but with *bruises*…. I was having strange hallucinations—the kind of things that occurred in my childhood but which, at the time, I thought was normal. After a serious bout of depression, I began seeing bizarre parapsychological phenomena exacerbated by the discovery of medieval books on alchemy and magic. Soon, I was sliding into a twilight zone wherein my sensibility was ambushed by these visual phenomena. I'd fallen prey to the charm of the paranormal and wanted to experiment further and yet, I was afraid: I saw the dangers ahead. ¶ *It was then that you met Dr. Bernhard?* ¶ Once again, it was a meeting that took place purely by chance, under the most natural circum-

Fellini in eighteenth-century lace sleeves handling phallic potatoes for the camera. (*Fellini's Casanova*, 1976)

stances…. [Ernst] Bernhard gave me the precious gift of Jungian psychology that helped me to interpret these paranormal events in a new light. My contact with the paranormal would produce an extreme excitation—especially with my temperament, which is similar to that of a vagabond in a fairy tale—and I placed these supernatural events on a mysterious, atmospheric plane, at once fantastic, irrational, fabulous but without a structure to give it meaning. This paranormal interpretation of reality—and the brutal aspect that often accompanied my experiences, which were conducted without a guide, without specific training or cultural references to fall back on—were slowly undermining my sanity. So, my encounter with Bernhard and Jung refocused my perception by showing me that a part of myself—the self that had become fanatical and arrogant—was precisely in tune with someone who wished only to believe in absurd, incomprehensible fantasies. Like the true sage he was, Bernhard didn't try to eliminate the charm of my parapsychological adventures. Instead, he tried to explain them using Jungian theories, teachings that could accommodate—rather than repudiate—my own mental processes. My interest in the paranormal is a natural inclination as evidenced in my profession as a filmmaker. ¶ *After 8 ½ and your encounter with Bernhard, one feels a liberation from neorealist principles, that now you consider filmmaking as an art form in which the director himself creates his film according to his own inner dictates and not those imposed on him by critics, producers, or the public.* ¶ Art is something that encourages us to remember or to imagine. After 8 ½, I had the satisfaction of experiencing what I had only imagined, encouraged in my belief that cinema could also express something that wasn't just reality photographed in a neorealist manner but in such a way that it possessed an authenticity, a faithfulness to life, that filmmaking could narrate inner realities—deeper, subtler reali-

Giant wind machines to create the illusion of a blizzard. (*Amarcord*, 1973)

ties—as Kurosawa or Buñuel had done. I felt that filmmaking could succeed in rendering everyday reality transparent and offer us a multitude of others.

ARTISTIC FREEDOM

I don't believe in total freedom for the artist. Left on his own, free to do anything he likes, the artist ends up doing nothing at all. If there's one thing that's dangerous for an artist, it's precisely this question of total freedom, waiting for inspiration and the rest of it. That's all romantic rhetoric. The production of *8 ½* taught me a great lesson. For two months, I worked on the script with Flaiano and Pinelli, but it wasn't convincing because I couldn't decide on what the protagonist did for a living—one day he was a writer, the next a journalist, then he was a lawyer.... Finally, I gave the order to start everything. My producer, Angelo Rizzoli, had given me total control of the production, trusting in my past success with *La Dolce Vita*. I ordered the decor of a farm built, I sketched the characters, I telephoned everybody but still I couldn't decide. I felt myself floundering; I was on the brink of abandoning the project. But I gave the order to start, that we begin *now* because someone or something is going to intervene to force me, to shame me into making this picture. The simple fact that I couldn't face telling my loyal troupe that I was about to abandon a film whose subject I knew nothing about revealed my subject to me: a director who no longer knows what film he wants to make.

Con man Picasso (Richard Basehart) loses his hat in a neorealist landscape. (*The Swindle*, 1955)

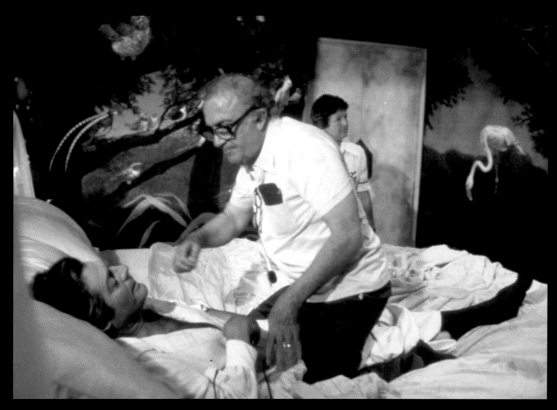

Getting it right: Fellini fine-tuning Marcello Mastroianni's makeup. (*City of Women*, 1980)

BALDNESS

The only advantage about going bald is that you get rid of dandruff by removing its hiding place.

BALTHUS

When I first met Balthus, the great French painter of Polish origin, we sat down together in the gardens of the Villa Medicis and he asked me to talk to him of beauty. For a moment, my mind went blank and then I recalled Stendhal's "la beauté est la promesse du bonheur" and that seemed to satisfy him until slowly he turned his noble face to fix me squarely in the eyes and asked, "Did you have trouble with your French when you made *The Clowns*?" ∫ "No," I replied. "But the French did."

BEGGING FOR MONEY

Ingmar Bergman's *Ansiktet*, or *The Face* [in America, *The Magician*], has an extraordinary sequence where Vogler, the protagonist played by Max von Sydow, has successfully performed his supernatural magic scene and descends the stairs begging for a handful of kronas. "Won't you pay me?" he says pathetically, with uniqueness of facial and verbal expression. It's a familiar refrain in the film industry and I identify with that kind of heart-destroying humiliation for services that were rendered in blood.

Fellini setting up shots for the famous passage of the *Rex*, a Fascist regime's technological marvel. (*Amarcord*, 1973)

BOCCIONI

[Fellini is shown one of his working drawings from *City of Women* for a fresco at the villa of Catzone ("Big Prick"): a naked Ethiopian woman in profile kowtows to a man with a cubist profile wearing a Fascist military cap. Written in Fellini's hand above the woman are the words, *cubista, Boccioni*.] ¶ *What significance does Boccioni have in this film?* ¶ I discovered Boccioni thanks to my colleague Brunello Rondi. He was an excellent cubist painter appreciated by the likes of Mussolini and so evokes a certain Fascist era and atmosphere that I needed in that particular sequence at Catzone's villa. In fact, Boccioni was instrumental in my idea of dividing my psyche into Marcello and Catzone in order to analyze myself in a more critical light. In Boccioni's work, every profile contains a plethora of profiles that one decomposes according to the *emotional atmosphere* he wishes to create and not to a rigorous process of predetermined lines and forms. What this cubist achieved on canvas gave me the impetus to see what I could do in a film using the same principles.

BORN LIAR

During the preparation of a filmed interview with Italo Calvino, the writer read to me a quotation he treasured: "The Sphinx is a masterpiece in the Sahara desert and cannot be described as anything other than an illusion. The Sphinx has not moved but the men who built it have all disappeared without a trace, like a midday mirage." It seems that you share this idea that art makes things real. ¶ I do. That's why I can't respond with precision to critics' requests for specific episodes, fragments of events that actually occurred in my life because the

ABOVE: The drive-in billboard of Anita (Anita Ekberg as the giantess) urging Italians to "Drink more milk!" (*The Temptations of Dr. Antonio*, 1962) OPPOSITE: Fellini indicating how a fantasy projection should strangle Juliet (Giulietta Masina). (*Juliet of the Spirits*, 1965)

things that are the most real for me are the ones I invented in my films. I think I was born on January 20, 1920, but as the poet said, "Nothing is known. Everything is imagined." Delacroix affirmed that the most tangible things for a painter are the illusions he creates on his canvas; the rest is air. That's what happened to the town I was born in. I can't deny the fact that I was born in Rimini but the real town has faded and been replaced by the Rimini of my films—*I Vitelloni, Amarcord*—down to the last detail. This deconstruction is much more a part of me, of my life, than the Rimini that exists topographically. So, I'm a born liar, that's the simple truth of the matter. ¶ *In response to my question "Are novelists liars?" Calvino replied: "Novelists tell the truth hidden at the bottom of every lie."* ¶ I always knew I had a robust reason for being the liar I am! Truth may be stranger than fiction but a lie is always more interesting. ¶ *Because it's more entertaining?* ¶ Because of what it reveals about the liar! ¶ *"I feel suspicious about writers who claim to tell the truth about themselves, about life, or about the world. I prefer contemplating the truths I find in writers who present themselves as the most bold-faced liars." These are Calvino's words and he might just as well have been talking about you.* ¶ Calvino's right. I think lies are the soul of cinema. Why is it necessary that the images we invent be credible? On the other hand, the emotion behind those images, underlying the dialogue, must be absolutely genuine. ¶ *The obligation to express, then, is focused on the invention of memories, of inventing the past.* ¶ I don't think it's possible to distinguish past, present, and future—the imagined past from recollections of what actually happened—as distinctly as we think it is. I tried dealing with that in *8 ½*. I think someone who tries to follow his vocation, as a storyteller, can't make this distinction at the moment he's creating his little universe. The creation of his world is a total one. His subsequent identification with it is

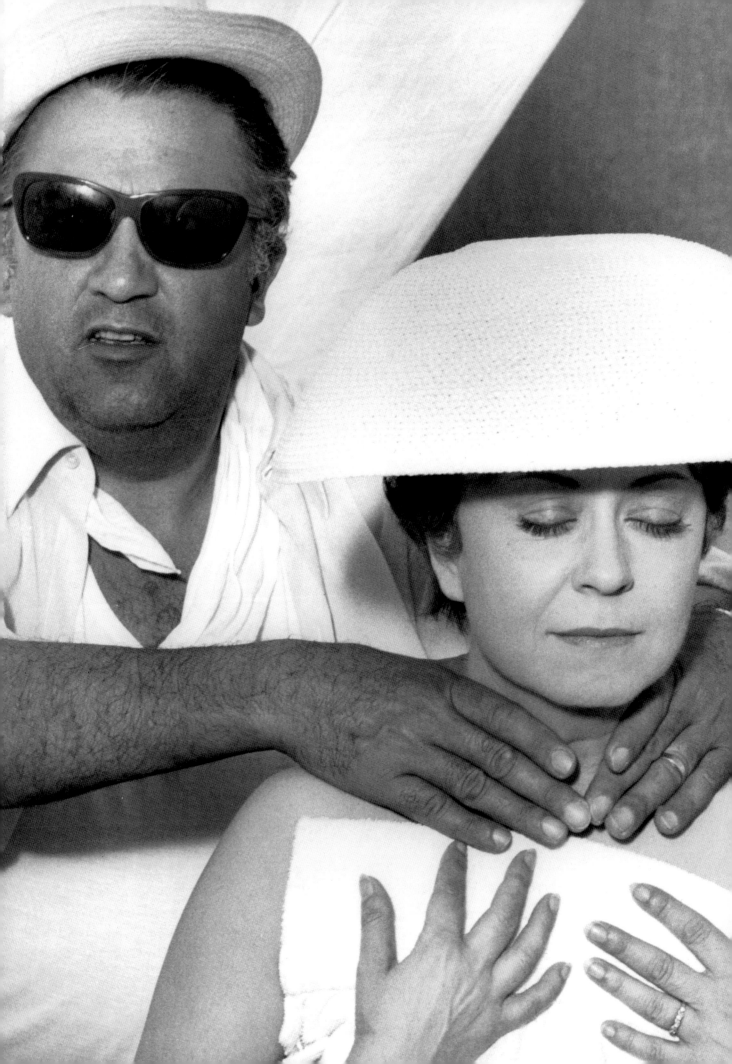

Receiving a lady's slipper in Susy's bordello-like bedroom. (*Juliet of the Spirits*, 1965)

total as well. ¶ *Why is the identification a total one?* ¶ Because you must absolutely believe in what you're making and when you believe in your creation, you identify with it. It becomes a universe complete in time and not limited to space or the description of characters. You see, my work is to make films and the way I make them is not just a mode of expression, it's a way of being. I identify so completely with the extroversion we call filmmaking that, outside the studio, beyond the refuge of the arc lamps, of the materialization of fantasies or dreams, of applying the actors' makeup, of the creation of an order however illusory, cut off from the atmosphere of the cinema set I feel empty, immediately in exile. Anything can happen to me so much do I feel out of tune with what we consider to be normal existence. I film and so I am. To arrive at the heart of a story in film is to reach the center of myself. ¶ *And having reached that center is Federico dissatisfied being Fellini?* ¶ No, no, I found a good deal of sympathy for myself. I have certainly had more than my fair share of fame and good fortune. The long narrative that a creator threads into the fabric of his work is the search, on various levels, for a style, a coherence, an essence, a greater spontaneity, to be more sincere, less conceptual, to live the expression itself. It's the search for the truest, the most authentic part of oneself. ¶ *How would you best describe yourself?* ¶ I am felliniesque. ¶ *You recognize "felliniesque" as the most authentic part of yourself?* ¶ Yes, because the adjective describes my work as a filmmaker. Creation is a unique way of appropriating the shadows, the sounds, the scents, the identity card, the images that reveal a man to himself and through which he can recognize a certain continuity over the passage of time. I'm giving you a rather existential point of view reduced to simple, concrete, and mundane terms. But it seems to me that even as a child this feeling of suspension, of waiting, the emotion procured in waiting for some-

Fanny (Sandra Milo), the circus performer conjured up by Juliet's
visionary faculties. (*Juliet of the Spirits*, 1965)

thing to happen, was embodied in a kind of echo, a sound, a suggestion with which I have always identified. I don't want to stress a mystical interpretation here. I'm talking about a state of mind, a daily outlook
in which this feeling of waiting never ceases. ¶ To say that I'm felliniesque, however, is to mouth only half
my self. I can't tell you what or where my true self lies within the boundaries of that adjective. The deepest
part of me identifies with the myth of Echo and Narcissus. For me, the two are merged into a single being
suspended in time. I'm Narcissus waiting for Echo waiting for Narcissus. I'm someone who believes in
anything that makes him wonder. I believe in everything—which is to believe in nothing—but I believe in
that, too, and I don't worry about the contradiction. I'm the King of Contradiction! Not to believe wearies
me. It's putting up barriers, establishing limits, becoming blocked about things that remain inexplicable
to me and to the so-called initiates. How much healthier it is to simply believe in it all. Why discriminate?
To believe is part and parcel of that vague yet fundamental sentiment in which I recognize an essential part
of myself—the feeling of waiting for something. Don't misunderstand me: I'm not stressing a mystical
interpretation of life. I'm talking about a state of mind, a daily outlook in which this sentiment of waiting
never leaves me. On the other hand, I haven't the slightest idea as to what it is I'm waiting for.

B

Free as a bird: Casanova (Donald Sutherland) escaping from
Venice's ghastly prison known as *I piombi* ("the lead plumbing").
(*Fellini's Casanova*, 1976)

Donald Sutherland (Casanova) discussing close-ups with Fellini. (*Fellini's Casanova*, 1976)

CASANOVA

It seemed to me that Donaldino's [Donald Sutherland] face was perfectly adapted to the image of an Italian who was unripe, juvenile, a kind of Pinocchio-in-the-uterus, which was the image I had of the real Casanova whom I considered a *stronzo* or fool, an idiot. Only a great professional actor like Sutherland could incarnate such negative qualities effectively. In addition, Don has fabulous blue eyes. As my Casanova, these eyes expressed the sterile masturbatory fantasies of the voyeur, of a walking sperm bank suffering from chronic insomnia. The real Casanova was never properly born, which is the meaning of the film's opening when the gigantic black head of Venus with staring, goitrous eyes rises to the surface of the Grand Canal as the carnival crowd chants, "Fornicating cunt, defecating ass, subterranean old hag, stinking old woman!" And then the pulleys snap. The great female head sinks to the bottom of the Venetian lagoon, like a miscarriage or an abortion. But her eyes never close: they remain fixed on the void, eyeless in Gaza. It's a film that cost me dearly. Every day for three years, I inspected the wrinkles of a thousand extras. Never worked so hard in my life. We were plagued by nothing but well-publicized accidents and catastrophes. Even the end of production had Don [Sutherland] collapsing in the field where we'd shot the last brief scene with Venice frozen in ice. Solemnly removing his false nose and chin, he walked out over the uneven field waving his huge black cape in a final salute when suddenly he disappeared. The heavy cape had dragged him down. He got up, waved, and fell down again. He was put through supernatural trials that would have discouraged the likes of Indiana Jones. ∫ *Why supernatural?* ∫ I'm convinced that the real Casanova was persecuting us for my having ruined his reputation. But what could I do? You can't imprison a ghost. ∫

Casanova (Donald Sutherland) dancing a duet in his mind on the frozen Grand Canal with a Hoffmanesque mechanical doll (Adele Lojodice). (*Fellini's Casanova*, 1976)

The film ends with Casanova in the arms of a mechanical doll that, at times, looks like a stylized version of La Masina *in the late 1950s. Is that just my perverse imagination?* ¶ Poor Guilietta! *Casanova* was the product of a director's disarming intention to take stock of his life and shout his discoveries over the rafters of Rome. The film taught me that the absence of love is the worst suffering anyone can endure.

CHERRIES AND PLASTIC SEAS

In the studio, everything is false just like in life because the more artificial an object is, the greater its reality. The bowl of cherries on your kitchen table look real whereas in the studio they look artificial. In the studio, when you design your own cherries, your own bowl, and your own table with great exactitude of expression, all this artifice contributes to your creation's looking real. Film the real sea and it looks false. Struggle to film a plastic sea of your own invention and that created reality becomes the more interesting one because it's a heightened reality linked to the power of suggestion—the very opposite of the hyperrealism of Hollywood's special effects. With a sheet, fifty pounds of Parmesan cheese and two technicians, you've got a blizzard. The magical, disappearing frescoes of *Roma* were made using what's known in the trade as "washable paint." When applied to a wall, it dries leaving a shiny transparent surface. Heating it, however, causes it to go opaque, brittle, and white. Rinaldo Geleng painted fake pillars with Roman frescoes and behind these we installed a heating system that resembled a series of radiators stacked on top of each other. The moment I shouted, "Action!" Rinaldo hit the mains and the effect was stupendous. We filmed it in four takes. It was a simple clever invention on a par with the mousetrap and

Studio twilight and black plastic oceans: satirizing an entire society for its false ideals. (*Amarcord*, 1973)

the fly swatter. So, as a creator, I'm dedicated to the idea of cinema as painting, of exploring a language of painting in film. I've gone beyond classic narrative techniques and psychological realism at the expense of losing the international public I won with *La Strada* and *La Dolce Vita*. But as everyone knows, the public is a fiction anyways.

CHOOSING AN ACTOR

I choose an actor in a very deliberate way since the story is incarnated in the faces. I start by making drawings of the characters as I imagine them. After the initial tits and ass stage, I publish a notice in the newspaper announcing the production of my new film and invite anyone who wants to see me to come around to my office. Then I audition the hundreds that show up and pin photographs of hundreds more on a large board in my office. As I say, the face has to coincide with the one I have in my mind, but I'm also open to new possibilities, to the unexpected. For example, sometimes I'll choose a face that has absolutely nothing to do with the one I've drawn and set out to find. But it works in the end because the result is more original than what I'd previously imagined.

CHURCHES

I never go to church. If you happen to find me inside one it's because I love looking at the paintings, the architecture, the statues. Italian churches have lots of dark, moldy corners and I find that irresistible.

"[T]he story is incarnated in the faces." Hiram Keller as Ascilto.
(*Fellini's Satyricon*, 1969)

CINEMA AND LITERATURE

Every work of art lives within the medium in which it was conceived and through which it expresses itself. Adapting a novel for cinema means transferring novelistic situations to another medium unsuited to its particular rhythms and cadences. Cinema doesn't need literature. Of course, there are magnificent exceptions that prove the rule such as Visconti's *Death in Venice,* but in this case, the director created another dimension to house Mann's novella. Visconti took a masterpiece to create a masterpiece using alembicated fancy as cinematic language so rarefied that his achievement is nothing short of alchemy.

CINEMA MACHINE

The tremendous success of *La Dolce Vita* gave me final cut: from then on I had absolute control of all my films. On the other hand, I could no longer offer a producer an intimate film with a modest budget, the kind I was making in the fifties, without his feeling humiliated. "What? You think I can't afford you?" he'd protest, snapping his fingers. "Why, I can shell out a billion lire for the next Fellini anytime, anywhere, anyplace!" The story didn't matter to him, what he wanted was to close a huge financial deal using my name when all I needed for my project was an eight hour a day, two-week shoot with four weeks for post-sync and dubbing. "Peanuts!" shouted this Napoleon of junk bonds. There was no escape: I had become a cinema machine.

CITY OF WOMEN

City of Women was a voyage into the feminine universe, constantly perceived through the eyes of an

Homage to Chaplin's "chalky mask" in a sequence inspired by Fellini's fond memories of Rome's vaudeville theater revues. (*Fellini's Roma*, 1972)

Italian male, vaguely macho, attracted, fascinated and frightened, a male version of Little Red Riding Hood lost in the forest. I think that's the meaning of the film: a voyage to discover the most secret part of oneself and of woman. It seems to me, quoting Jung, that man projects onto woman the obscure part of himself, thereby making her a fascinating creature. The female is the unknown planet, the part the male wishes to unite with in order to achieve a wholeness, a sphericity, an integrity, and for the same reason, it's the dark side of himself that attracts and yet intimidates him. ¶ *Could we say that the felliniesque woman is a projection of your own image?* ¶ That's something I won't admit! I hear it expressed often enough and you repeat it but, surely, *Madame Bovary, c'est moi*.

CLOWNS

Garbo had a judge's mask, glacial like a ghost's, a kind of female version of the Pope. Chaplin's was a White Clown's face not altogether innocent because it played on your affections. He's like a sleepwalker, at once haunted and haunting. I'm very fond of Garbo, but my loyalty lies with the great comedians and it's been that way since childhood. Comedians like our Toto, whose smile recalled the Messenger of Death, or Buster Keaton, the *ballerino*—they're my favorites because I consider them as the benefactors of humanity. Clowns do us a world of good and making people laugh is my true vocation.

CONFORMITY

An artist is fundamentally a transgressor. He can also be a revolutionary but psychologically, an artist has a

Vernacchio (Fanfulla), ancient Rome's cruelest clown. (*Fellini's Satyricon*, 1969)

child's need to transgress. For this, his parents, a priest, the police, an interviewer, are enough. A creator needs to express himself by an act of transgression in order to undermine tradition, the status quo, of what is accepted, of the conformity that stifles him because it's already outdated. In short, he needs an enemy.

CONTRACTS

I make a film because I sign a contract, they give me an advance, I don't want to give it back and so I have to make the film. My psychological makeup is probably derived from the fifteenth-century artist who needed a pope, an archduke, a prince, someone who says to him in sinister tones, "Paint me a fresco on this ceiling!" or "Write me a madrigal for my sister's wedding!" The court artist, flattered and subsequently threatened with having his hands chopped off, was obliged to create to fulfill a commission. In a similar way, it seems to me that my films are born because I sign a contract and then I'm harassed and threatened. I'm the kind of artist who needs a patron, not just to supply him with commissions but, more importantly, a figure he can rebel against, someone he can fear. It's part of film legend that the director loathes his producer, considering him nothing more than a businessman and beneath contempt. The producer starts legal proceedings claiming his director's a spendthrift megalomaniac who enjoys prolonging the battle—and I'm no exception. But I have to confess that I thrive on this opposition, on having someone who irritates me, who contradicts everything I say to the point where I'm forced to defend

Recreating childhood memories of the circus and a visual metaphor of man's place in the world. (*The Clowns*, 1970)

Fellini mimes the scene in which Titta's father (Armando Brancia) returns home after being beaten by Fascists. (*Amarcord*, 1973)

CRAFTSMANSHIP

I discovered that what's really important for a creator isn't what we vaguely define as inspiration or even what it is we want to say, recall, regret, or rebel against. No, what's important is the way to say it. Art is all about craftsmanship. Others can interpret craftsmanship as style if they wish. Style is what unites memory or recollection, ideology, sentiment, nostalgia, presentiment, to the way we express all that. It's not what we say but how we say it that matters. ❡ Of all artistic forms and expressions, cinema is the one that resembles life the most. It requires exactitude, a unique respiration, gestures and attitudes of mathematical precision. Expressing a dream, a fantasy, is an operation of advanced mathematics, like physics. It's like launching a rocket into space. Whatever it is you want to express artistically deserves the maximum of rigor possible. Anything less is betrayal. A filmmaker's greatest enemy is compromise. Life is meticulous so how can an artistic expression be otherwise? An artist has the possibility of making something more real than reality itself. Life appears to us as governed by chance but it is nothing if not exact. Approximation irritates me. A green must be exactly a particular shade of green, just as it is for a painter, and a face must be precisely that particular face, capable of expressing what it must express the moment it appears on screen. Once you begin approximating your vision, there's no end to the damage. ❡ *Would you say you're a perfectionist?* ❡ I would. ❡ *But you seem almost too impatient to be one.* ❡ My closest collaborators tell me I'm impatient, that it's a flaw in my character. I don't agree at all and get very impatient with them.

CREATION

A created thing is never invented and it is never true: it is always and ever itself.

Directing Pupella Maggio (Titta's mother) to explode with anger after losing patience with mad Uncle Teo stuck in a tree. (*Amarcord*, 1973)

CURIOSITY

Curiosity is something to cultivate if we expect to survive. It gives you a kind of alibi, the strength to continue. You know, I once stayed in a large psychiatric hospital for women in Magliano as a voluntary patient—I repeat voluntary—to conduct research for a film I wanted to do. This was more than thirty years ago. Enclosed within the four walls of this kind of city of mad women, I felt strangely free. It gave me a sense of freedom impossible to describe, but which was based on the reality created by the unfettered imagination, the reality each of us can see if we try to peer over the walls of our personal prisons. So perhaps curiosity can justify a life: to observe and to discover. Are you pessimistic? ¶ *Yes.* ¶ But in any case, Damiano, what else can we do except to observe with affection and irony, and try to do only what we are capable of doing, what we do with pleasure.

CUTS

I like making one- or two-second cuts in my films. If you look closely at *And the Ship Sails On*, you'll discover a series of very short cuts made usually in the middle of a scene. For example, in the scene where Orlando, played by Freddie Jones, enters his cabin and addresses the camera, he shuts the door behind him and suddenly the entire scene tilts for a split second. The public assumes that they're watching an old and scratchy copy when in truth those cuts are deliberate. They are my signature. ¶ *Do you ever need to isolate yourself during a film shoot?* ¶ No, I don't make films holed up in a monastery! ¶ *What about when you're writing a script?* ¶ I put the finishing touches to the script of *La Dolce Vita* in a hotel in Fregene with Tullio Pinelli and Ennio Flaiano over several weeks.... I would say that some of my ideas, characters, dialogue,

OPPOSITE: Fellini directing the Church procession that has come to spread the word of God to prostitutes on the Passeggiata Archeologica. (*The Nights of Cabiria*, 1957) ABOVE: Sylvia (Anita Ekberg) preparing to place a kitten on her head in the famous scene where she discovers the Trevi Fountain. (*La Dolce Vita*, 1959)

come to me when I'm in a car or on a train. At the time when I had a car, I used to go anywhere at anytime just to look at the trees, the sky, the colors, the faces that passed by in silence. Once I had two or three ideas, I'd stop by the roadside and write them down. ¶ *Is your method at all similar to a kind of automatic writing in the sense that the scene is rehearsed and then a rush of various ideas and attitudes suggest themselves to you?* ¶ Automatic writing is linked to an unconscious abandon, and as far as I know I'm not a surrealist. My method was discovered during *La Dolce Vita* and developed to my satisfaction in *8 ½*—the film where I learned how to write the script on the set itself. The life I depict in *The Voice of the Moon* and the family relationships I established—this fellow was the uncle, this boy the nephew, this girl the daughter—once created, are then observed with enormous attention to detail, a deliberate awareness that leaves nothing to chance. You know from day one where it is you have to get to and you discover, in the dark, what you need to get there. It's when everything is clear, defined, laid out in front of you, that you lose your way. ¶ *A completed scenario would only hamper the vitality you create on the set?* ¶ At the risk of appearing immodest, I have to confess that scripts, ideas, stories, dialogue, the tall dark stranger, his gun, and the beautiful blonde are useless to me. I want, need, to take risks in the dream laboratory called Cinecittà. I've always taken risks, even as far back as *The White Sheik*, *La Strada*, *Nights of Cabiria*, when I was using the streets as my lab. Flaiano, Pinelli, and I collaborated on a script, a producer was brought in, and I shot the film each day with the aim of being open and receptive to chance circumstances, to whatever and whoever might contribute to the vitality of the scene I was shooting. It's in my nature to take risks. Why should I change at this late stage?

A disillusioned and cynical Marcello (Marcello Mastroianni) during the orgy sequence. (*La Dolce Vita*, 1959)

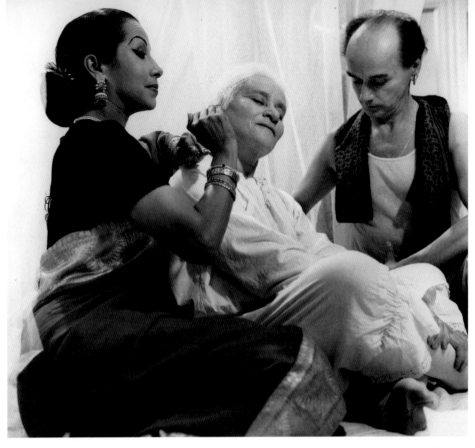

Bhisma (Valeska Gert), the androgynous witch-guru to whom the troubled Juliet has come for marital advice. (*Juliet of the Spirits*, 1965)

DAILIES

I find it dangerous to watch dailies because it usually has a pernicious influence on the following day's work. It's useful for spotting technical errors, but I consider these as beneficial accidents that underline the film's vitality.

DEATH

Everyone knows that time is Death, that Death hides in clocks. Imposing another time powered by the Clock of the Imagination, however, can refuse his law. Here, freed of the Grim Reaper's scythe, we learn that pain is knowledge and all knowledge pain. ¶ For a certain time now, the idea of dying has become more and more present. And yet, by chance, I'm blessed with a particular psychological mechanism in which happiness, worry, fear, debts, obligations, are all transformed into material for a story. I think it's due to the lucky cynicism of the creative type. In other words, that you've been put on this earth for the sole purpose of telling stories to amuse people. It's a monstrous form of narcissism, I know.... So, even the idea of dying—which would be inconvenient—is only a stimulus for the imagination. In this way, then, I think that an author's work can be witness to life's progression, of the diverse periods he's lived through among which are physical decline, advancing old age, the possibility of no longer existing—of no longer doing this interview—of being surrounded by friends who've come so far and waited so long to share these moments.... A creator's psychological makeup has the impudence of turning everything into a story. Death is something we all talk about in a literary way; we never discuss it as though it's real. We can invent a

Fellini and La Masina on the set of the TV variety show "We Proudly Present!," with director of photography, Tonino Delli Colli (standing) and *I Vitelloni*'s Fausto (Franco Fabrizi), the garish master of ceremonies. (*Ginger and Fred*, 1985)

thousand imaginary representations. We can have read all the testimonials. But, in the end, it's something that we will never truly grasp.

THE DECLINE OF CINEMA

I'm very pessimistic because I think the public has no sympathy for the big screen anymore. But I don't want to repeat the usual reasons behind the public's disaffection: television, fear of going out at night, the appalling conditions of Italy's movie theaters. The public has lost the habit of movie-going because the cinema no longer possesses the charm, the hypnotic charisma, the authority it once commanded. The image it once held for us all—that of a dream we dreamt with our eyes open—has disappeared. Is it still possible that one thousand people might group together in the dark and experience the dream that a single individual has directed?

DELIRIUM

What place, if any, does delirium have in your working life? ¶ I make a film as if I have a disease, suffering hot and cold sweats on an hourly basis, hovering constantly between ecstasy and anguish, lucidity and confusion. Everything is done in a kind of fever. Once the film is over, I fool myself into thinking I'm cured. Directing is a release of creative tension and energy that places me at the top of my form. I'm blessed, at ease with myself and it seems that all I need is sex. I exist; I live my dream that is the reality of the film. My tedious daily problems return once the film is over and I go on complaining until I'm back in the studio again.

Fellini showing the proper way to eat spaghetti for the outdoor trattoria sequence based on his memories and fantasies of prewar Rome. (*Fellini's Roma*, 1972)

DICTATOR DIRECTOR

An actress once denounced me to the press as a dictator director, that working with me was like taking orders from Stalin. She never met Stalin so how could she have followed his orders? And besides, Cinecittà isn't a gulag.

DIETS

I went on a diet for three months and all I took off was my hat. But I'm determined to win the battle of the bulge: it's a simple question of mind over platter.

DISENCHANTMENT

I leave my apartment in the morning and go for an espresso at Canova's. I stare out the window and watch the people hurrying to and fro. It's the same street I've known for the past forty years. But there's no more purity. No one is genuine. No one dreams any longer.

DORIAN GRAY

Did Wilde's Portrait of Dorian Gray *inspire you in some way when you conceived the monster fish at the end of* La Dolce Vita? *A monster that perhaps reflects Marcello's—and society's—final degradation?* ¶ *Dorian Gray* is an inspiration to us all, but the fish was inspired by a childhood memory of a giant jelly-like ray washed up on the beach in Rimini during a storm. If I comment on anything more, I'll simply limit the possible inter-

Cabiria (Giulietta Masina) making her appearance at the Kit Kat Club, a visual composition inspired by Fellini's drawings of Gelsomina for *La Strada*. (*The Nights of Cabiria*, 1957)

pretations. I make a film in the same way that I dream. A dream is a receptacle of esoteric truths, precious secrets: it remains fascinating as long as we preserve its air of mystery. Explaining a dream destroys its reason for being. Since images are the basis of my work, they should be capable of communicating the necessary emotions, including mysterious and contradictory meanings.

DRAWINGS AS GUIDES TO A FILM

I've always had the tendency to scribble on a blank surface. It's a habit I've kept whenever I prepare a new film. A film takes shape with the help of these drawings by suggesting a certain perspective, situating the decor, visualizing the characters and their clothes. The character of Gelsomina in *La Strada* first came to me in the image of a little clown suddenly popping its head up from behind a theater curtain. *La Dolce Vita* was partly inspired by a dress in vogue in the late fifties. It was very chic and elegant but resembled a bag that covered up a woman's body. It occurred to me that the woman wearing it could be this ravishing creature, pure and full of life on the outside but inside, she was a skeleton of solitude and vice. For *8 ½*, I drew a giant woman dancing on a beach in front of a tiny naked boy with dark eyes and an erection. Near the woman's right arm, I pasted a newspaper photo of the Pope.

DREAMS

You've explained that you don't differentiate between everyday reality and the reality of dreams. This faith in dreams led you to keep a set of dream notebooks for over thirty years now. ¶ I began drawing my dreams after

Sylvia (Anita Ekberg) exulting with the Pan-like
Frankie Stout (Alan Dijon). (*La Dolce Vita*, 1959)

Eliminating the borderline between fact and fiction, dream and imagination. (*Fellini's Satyricon*, 1969)

my encounter with Dr. Ernst Bernhard, the famous Jungian psychoanalyst, but in actual fact I was keeping a record as a child. I tried sketching them down on pieces of crinkled paper, across notebook covers, but never in a systematic way. After meeting Bernhard and reading Jung, I took up the habit I'd abandoned and rediscovered the pleasure in narrating an amusing dream and attempting to fix it figuratively on the page with pencils and watercolors. It's a complicated business because the language of dreams, whether it is on the narrative or figurative level, is basically an impossible language. It demands a different code of expression that belongs to another dimension where reason and intellect are totally excluded. ¶ *Then how do you express your dreams?* ¶ Oneiric expression is done with symbols. The symbol thus becomes the most inclusive of languages. The images in my films are based on this research. ¶ *Would you say that it's an absolute world of symbols?* ¶ Yes, above all in the fundamental search for meaning. ¶ *A sort of quest for the meaning of life?* ¶ Yes, through art. Art is a necessity, an interpretation of life, which, if left to itself, is probably devoid of meaning—monstrous. Art, on the other hand, is something that offers comfort, reassures us, speaks to us in highly protective terms. It forces us to meditate on life and on man who, without art, is nothing more than a beating heart, a stomach that digests, lungs that breathe, hands that strike the air, eyes that fill up with images stripped of all meaning. I believe that art is the most successful attempt to inculcate in man the indispensable need for a life of the spirit, which only art—no matter what art—is capable of expressing. ¶ *Have some of your dreams appeared in your films?* ¶ Yes, but always transformed from their original state. The language of dreams is that of film and film is a dream. You can dilate space, create ellipses in time, make people appear and disappear for no apparent reason. When you recall a

Sylvia (Anita Ekberg) on set in the stairs leading up to Saint Peter's, dressed in the strange but sexy equivalent of a priest's habit. (*La Dolce Vita*, 1959)

dream, you remember bizarre perspectives and characters but above all, a quality of light impossible to describe, the kind associated with a free conscience. Since this light both reveals and conceals our deepest emotions, I try to reproduce it in the studio in the hope that I can make my films "dreamable."

DUBBING

An actor's voice has no importance for me because a director must exert absolute control over the entire film, including the sound. I remove the actor's original voice and replace it with the same voice recording the definitive dialogue that's written after the final shoot. Dubbing arranges everything, as in music, like a film score. The non-correspondence between the words spoken and the actor's lip movements usually annoy the technicians but that has nothing to do with me. It's a laboratory problem.

OPPOSITE: Alter ego: Marcello Mastroianni as Guido Anselmi, the director in search of a film. (*8 ½*, 1963) ABOVE: Fellini's paternal grandmother, Francesca Lombardini (1860–1938), affectionately described as the "Indian brave."

8 ½

The story decides the structure and since a story must have characters, these characters impose a specific narrative structure. So some of my films have stories that require a freer, more "open" form or sometimes a labyrinthine structure, both of which suggest dreamlike narratives. In *And the Ship Sails On*, I employed a linear narration more suited to myth and tragedy that, instead of impeding the flow of emotions, only serves to heighten the mounting sense of anguish. But the *shape of the story* that turned out to be *8 ½*, its form and style, is what attracted me, made me want to tell the story in the first place. Form is never more important than content: the two go hand in hand. ¶ There is a contest going on between the filmmaker that is me and the filmmaker in the film, between the thing created and its creator. That constant tension throughout is why it's a good film. ¶ I don't think *8 ½* is an enigmatic film because the expression had to be realized in its entirety. In *8 ½*, a part of the story, or a character, or a portion of the landscape only appears enigmatic to the spectator, that is, hidden like a figure in the carpet. But what seems enigmatic was secreted unconsciously and forms an organic whole in the film: I didn't consciously set out to tease the viewer, to leave him perplexed or mystified. If the enigmatic exists, it's there because it couldn't be helped: it's not deliberate but inevitable.

EPIPHANIES

I was a solitary child, vulnerable, withdrawn, skinny, and subject to fainting spells. So in order to give some color to my cheeks, I spent summers with my grandmother, Franceschina, in Gambettola. She was a very handsome woman who looked like an Indian brave. One day, playing in the fields, I discovered that I could transcribe colors into sounds; that I could color sound. I was seated under a poplar and I heard a cow lowing in the barn. Immediately, I saw something coming out of the barn wall, undulating like a tongue, a wing—a red carpet—flying slowly in the air. It passed through me then disappeared like a huge fan of microscopic rubies scintillating in the sun. It was then that I felt I was the poplar with roots in the ground and branches in the sky: I was outside myself, outside my own humanity and for an instant I felt a cold shiver of belonging to the animal world. It was a sensation of profound silence, of extraterrestrial colors. Naturally, it's the kind of experience that, when acknowledged, makes people question your mental respectability. But without a doubt, it was this childhood epiphany that determined my propensity for the fantastic, the unknown, for all that is enigmatic.

EXPEDITIONS

My films are stuffed with sequences that, for lack of a better term, I call "Expedition Scenes." *The Voice of the Moon*, for example, opens in a marshy landscape with Ivo Salvini [Roberto Benigni] a captive to the strange voices he hears emanating from a well, which isn't surprising: he's just been released from a mental hospital. Suddenly, he sees a group of men marching in Indian file behind him and chanting, "The cunt! The cunt! The cunt!" Intrigued, he accompanies them on an expedition to an isolated villa where they spy on a frowsy middle-aged woman performing a decidedly chaste striptease in front of a TV set that's spewing nothing but static. Well, this sequence has its origins in *The Free Women of Magliano*, an abandoned project from the fifties based on the book by Mario Tupino. Roberto, the young protagonist, is a doctor undergoing a spiritual and moral crisis who decides to spend a year in a mental hospital. He soon makes friends with a few colleagues and one of the many sequences I developed for this film was their expedition to the nearby Montecantini Hotel where the chambermaid, the rumor goes, is an absolute knockout. One evening after work, they hop into Roberto's noisy Alfa Romeo and tear out to Montecantini. It's off-season, however, and the hotel is closed. The chambermaid with the fabulous breasts and big fat ass, vaunted by the asylum's doctors, is nowhere to be found. So they wake up the caretaker, forcing him to give them the young woman's address: she's the daughter of peasants who find work in the fields when the hotel's shut down over the winter. The grotesque, lunatic search for the body of an idealized woman continues well into the early hours until they arrive at a pitiful rundown farm, lost in the sticks. Here, in the dead wintry silence, facing mute and shuttered windows, their feverish lust evaporates. As dawn breaks, they have no choice but to return to the mental hospital of Magliano.

EXPERIENCE

Experience is what you get while looking for something else.

EXPRESSING ONESELF

I don't think an artist is capable of expressing himself except in his own language and that's why I could never accept all the film proposals offered to me by American producers. I can't deny the fact that I'm Italian, profoundly Italian, having been educated and spent my whole life here. I could never go and film, for example, in the American desert like Antonioni did in *Zabriskie Point*. I can film only through the filter of memory that decants, decomposes, burrows into the heart of things. I don't seem to understand anything in a foreign country and I return weighed down with useless information. Abroad, I'm blind.

opposite: Fellini directing Magali Noël (La Gradisca) in a Fascist fantasy sequence. (*Amarcord*, 1973) above: Fascism on the march: a film based on isolation, dream, torpor, and ignorance. (*Amarcord*, 1973)

FASCISM

Amarcord is the reflection of an incapacity to critically observe our Fascist past, a past we reject but which we can never be separated from: what shapes your past invariably shapes an intimate part of you. So *Amarcord* is more a diagnostic of the present than it is nostalgia. In fact, when *Satyricon* first came out, many saw it as a commentary on May 1968. I think films such as *Casanova* or *And the Ship Sails On* can be interpreted as reflecting a certain actuality just as much as the prime-time news report.

FIDELITY

It's easier to be faithful to a restaurant than it is to a woman.

FILM CRITICS

No critic writing about a film could say more than the film itself, although they do their best to make us think the opposite.

FILMMAKERS

You once said that you'd never seen any films by Flaherty so why should you see those by Coppola. A bit nasty, don't you think? ¶ What I meant was that it's irritating having someone ask you if you've seen any of your colleagues' films as if there's some kind of tacit obligation among filmmakers to see each other's work. Imagine Coppola's reply to a critic's question, "Francis Ford, have you seen Fellini's *8½*?" Francis Ford: "Why should I see *8½* when I've never seen Godard's *One + One*?"

Wanda Cavalli (Brunella Bovo) in dispute with the jealous wife of the White Sheik (Alberto Sordi) on a beach in Fregene. (*The White Sheik*, 1952)

FILMMAKING

What is so difficult in filmmaking is trying to go beyond one's own personal psychology to the frontiers of myth, inventing images that possess universal myth motifs, archaic residues, whose content is collective and not exclusively personal, with the hope of projecting these images straight into the filmgoer's psyche. Obviously, I admire those filmmakers who attempt to exploit the shape of the fable in their films. Filmmaking is akin to the creation of a new religion, a great psychic system of healing. A genuine filmmaker is not only interested in entertaining his audience—and this is going to sound even more presumptuous—he also needs to affect them in a profound way, *to effect a change in them* by making them question the reality of their times. Cinema is not about delivering messages but about raising questions. Its ultimate goal is Socratic in nature. I think it's clear that future generations of filmmakers will build on what Buñuel, Kubrick, Bergman, and Kurosawa have given us.

FLASH GORDON

In Florence in the late thirties, I wrote scenarios to *Flash Gordon* while working for the publisher, Nerbini. Mussolini had banned American comic books and so we found, as we often do in Italy, a solution that suited everyone: the Italian Ministry of Popular Culture agreed that we could finish the scenarios previously launched at great expense provided we worked exclusively with Italians. So I collaborated on a few episodes. Giove Toppi handled the drawings, I wrote the text, introducing a particular *romagnolo* flavor that wasn't present in Alex Raymond's original work. We were paid ten lire a week and when the series took off, Nerbini doubled our salaries to ten lire every two weeks! ¶ Much later, while working with Milo Manara on *Voyage to Tulum*, I discovered that there's no difference, relatively

Alberto Sordi as the White Sheik in Fellini's debut as an independent director, set in the world of the "photo-novel." (*The White Sheik*, 1952)

speaking, between making a film and making a comic strip: it demands the same logistical organization, the same imperious deadlines, the same solutions to laboratory problems, and above all, the same modes of expression. The animated film, as Calvino so clearly understood, is a metaphorical and metonymic art linked to spoken and onomatopoeic language. A film, as everyone knows, is a series of tiny boxes inside which you express a situation involving characters arranged in space where light and shadow, perspective and volume, are carefully worked out. The story progresses as these tiny boxes are set in motion. With a comic strip, you're dealing with the same tiny boxes except that they're frozen on a page. They possess a spectral fascination like the hunter's moose head on the wall in the study, like puppets without strings or butterflies pinned on a board. It's highly suggestive because the reader must imagine the movement from one frame to the next. In a certain sense, comic book expression is artistically purer than cinema in that it can't be defined, it's more allusive, less dependent on reality. This probably sounds strange coming from an ex-neorealist but right now I'm going through my neocartoonist phase.

THE FULGOR

It's well known that the Fulgor Cinema in Rimini is where I first discovered films as a child. Once, when I'd gone to see Valentino in *The Sheik* for the seventh time, a stunning Rubenesque blonde showed up just before the screening and handed the usher two tickets. "Where's the other person?" asked the usher. ❡ "Well," said the blonde, blushing through her makeup, "one seat is uncomfortable for me so I purchased two." ❡ "*Che culo!*" the cheeky usher replied. "Your seats are numbers thirty-four and fifty-three."

GENIUS

Nietzsche claimed that his genius was in his nostrils and I think that is a very excellent place for it to be.

GIULIETTA MASINA

For me, Giulietta will always be the projection of wounded innocence that in the end triumphs.

GIUSEPPE ROTUNNO

My cameraman, Peppino Rotunno, once told me that working together was like "being seated at a table in a Rimini café in winter" and I couldn't agree more. Both of us are *vitelloni* telling stories about last summer's holidays in order to prepare those of next summer. Our working day begins at 7 A.M. We meet at my flat at Cinecittà near Studio 5. I prepare coffee for us, scrape some Parmesan onto a plate, and we talk about everything except the work ahead of us. By eight o'clock, we're in the studio. We begin working separately and then meet to discuss our results. For example, Peppino sets up the morning's shots while I inspect the decor with a view to last-minute changes thought up the night before during my usual bout of insomnia. Once these changes are in place, I have Peppino arrange the necessary lighting and we start shooting a series of tests until lunch break. Work resumes without a break until six o'clock. During that time, I shoot from as many different camera angles as possible, all angles decided on and framed by myself, and together we resolve the numerous problems in perspective, volume, color, and lighting. Problems are sometimes easily resolved: by moving ever so slightly a five-hundred-watt projector and lighting another behind it, the sensation of anguish created earlier in the studio disappears and the set is bathed in a comforting, tranquil atmosphere. Ours is very much a push-and-pull relationship: I'm constantly pushing reality toward falsity whereas Peppino, by nature, is constantly pulling falsity toward reality. These two equal and opposite reactions create what has come to be my hallmark: the felliniesque, a distinctive style made with light, and where Peppino is my light.

GOD

God may not play dice but he enjoys a good round of *Trivial Pursuit* every now and again.

GUILT

You cannot love a person who makes you feel guilty all the time.

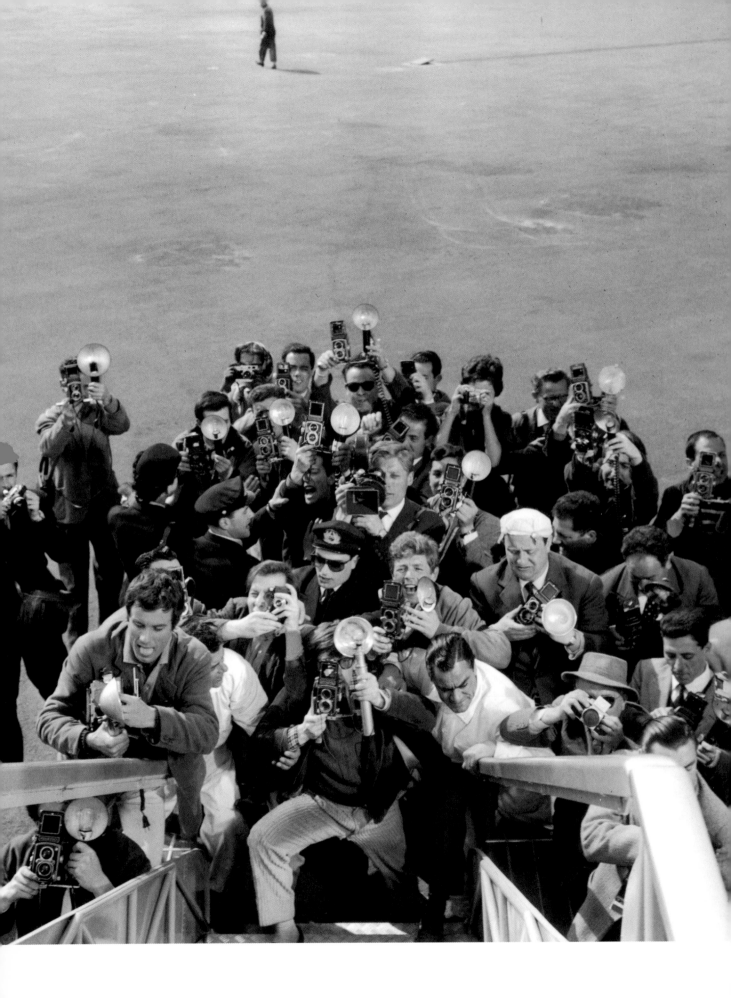

HOLLYWOOD

Of the many proposals put to me, I'd accepted to make a film portrait of America on the condition of being able to reconstruct it in a studio over here—I don't mean reconstructing the entire country, because even Studio 5, which is huge, couldn't contain it all. But at the time, Sherry Lansing, who was a beautiful and intelligent woman and an important figure at 20th Century Fox, understood this necessity to rebuild everything at Cinecittà and she tried convincing the administration to have me film two stories by Raymond Chandler. Above all, she wanted me to try to reconstruct memories of my own adventures in America, of unforgettable moments like visiting peep shows in Times Square with Groucho Marx, writing gags for Sid Caesar, hunting for arrowheads from a Cadillac along miles of dusty back roads, then driving out to Pacific Palisades to observe the shyness of turtles, getting hassled by television executives to adapt *The Divine Comedy* with George Burns as Dante, Mae West as Beatrice, and Lew Wasserman as God, things like that. It didn't work out. So I proposed making a film based on a day trip to Disneyland that is really the reflection of a puerile, vulgar, violent, and yet curiously sympathetic America where thousands of families converge. The film could have been shot in a journalistic, impressionistic manner, caustic but fair, in keeping with my colleague Paul Mazursky, who depicts the follies of his fellow Americans with a wry and affectionate sense of humor. That didn't work out, either. But it's too late for me to be thinking of transplanting myself to Hollywood. Groucho suggested I ought to go to Texas. "That's where men are men and women are women," he said, teasing me about my voice. "You should fit in someplace."

HYPE

I would love to make a film without being obliged to promote it afterward. I loathe having to talk about something you've taken two years or more to bring into existence only to have it drowned in your own hype. Hype is the awkward and desperate attempt to convince journalists that what you've made is worth the misery of having to review it. My films are based on fragile, half-digested ideas propped up with contradictory information and infused with nonexistent memories. If I'm lucky, I manage to get a few laughs. Films are made in the same way department stores sell off their woolens and trousers. It's like having a garage sale: I simply liquidate my limited stock of ideas that are focused exclusively on my provincial background, a lost childhood I'm forever reinventing.

HYPOCRISY

If I'm a cruel satirist at least I'm not a hypocrite: I never judge what other people do. Neither a politician nor a priest, I never censor what others do. Neither a philosopher nor a psychiatrist, I never bother trying to analyze or resolve my fears and neuroses. If I did, I'd no longer have reasons for making a film. Directing is the sole and unique way of healing myself, a celluloid therapy that keeps me sane.

Mutants of music: Fellini directing Roberto Benigni
(Ivo Salvini) at a disco of Dantesque proportions.
(*The Voice of the Moon*, 1990)

Fellini on set having his palm read: "I believe in anything that makes me wonder." (*Fellini's Casanova*, 1976)

I CHING

I once offered Tullio [Pinelli] a copy of the *I Ching, or Book of Changes*—he's as superstitious as I am although he makes a very convincing Cartesian. Flaiano, on the other hand, wouldn't have been caught dead reading such a book. Tullio and I spent entire afternoons on his Rome terrace like happy children playing with stalks of yarrow and getting remarkable results by sheer coincidence or by synchronicity, whichever you prefer. It was an exercise I introduced onto the set so as to encourage the *instinct of facility*: to let go while still directing with an iron hand. It's a kind of sober euphoria that relaxes the natural impulse to consciously interfere in what you're doing the moment you're doing it: you develop subconscious methods of ordering the inner chaos that feeds your artistic drives.

THE IMAGE

The image is the essential component of film. What else could it possibly be? If I were to ask you, what is the essential element of painting, what would you reply? Light, tonality…. ¶ *Yes, but there's also the question of culture, of a visual predisposition. An image isn't something neutral, is it?* ¶ An image that expresses an idea, a sentiment, an atmosphere, a recollection, and which suggests something to the spectator that regards not only the actor but the spectator as well. It seems to me that it's an image dense in meaning and that represents the soul of film. Without light, you don't have an image and without the image, you don't have cinema. Light is everything. It expresses ideology, emotion, color, depth, style. It can efface, narrate, describe. With the proper lighting, the ugliest face, the most idiotic expression, can radiate beauty or intelligence. In my work, dialogue is of little importance when compared to light and image.

IMPROVISATION

I don't think the word *improvisation* has any bearing on the creative process. It's a word I consider utterly inadequate, even irritating. No, I wouldn't speak of improvisation here, I'd use other terms: *la disponibilità* or receptivity, being open-minded. I would say that it's necessary to be receptive, open, responsive, to the thing that is trying to get born but which is still unformed and magma-like, confused, undefined. The creator is there to materialize it, to help define it, to suggest a certain confused world or a particular dimension. Any artist, who is called upon to paint a painting, compose an opera, write a novel, or direct a film, must maintain a certain availability, what I would call receptivity. That's the word, not improvisation. He must give himself up entirely to the phantom or creature that slowly begins to appear. An artist mustn't become entangled in the pretension of wanting to shape the creature exactly as he had first imagined it according to the parameters, the rules of his culture or his own ignorance, his political or aesthetic ideology. No, he must surrender, confident, to the suggestions that the creature will offer him, even during the most difficult moments such as the unexpected illness of a key actor on whom he can no longer depend, or the violent but inevitable dispute with the producer, or the fact that the director falls ill himself. He can interpret all of these events as impeding the vital flow of the film but, also, as necessary evils that force him to make changes, transformations, improvements that he would never have thought of had he not been possessed of this receptivity, this particular ear and eye attuned to the process that slowly defines itself day after day. The artist knows a work of art will achieve its full effect if it creates the impression of its having been excited into existence with miraculous suddenness. I didn't say that: Nietzsche did.

INSURANCE

Being naughty is like health insurance: the older you get the more it costs.

ITALIAN CINEMA

You know, Italy is a nation that still remains to be narrated in films. Italian cinema is guilty because it has never managed to express Italy. The same for Italian literature: we are a completely unknown race because of this. Perhaps Rome has been told a little. Naples, too, but only in a folkloric way. Sicily is forever seen in terms of its truculent Mafioso history. But the rest of Italy—the real Italy where every fifty kilometers there's witness of another culture, of different myths and customs—goes untold and that's unfortunate because, really, it's an unbelievable country.

IVO SALVINI

If you look closely, you'll see in various scenes throughout *The Voice of the Moon* a carefully veiled homage to Marcel Carnet's masterpiece, *Les Enfants du paradis.* The protagonist, Ivo Salvini, is a Pierrot not unlike the Pierrot of Carnet's film played by Jean-Louis Barrault, and a distant cousin to Gelsomina. Like me, he's a bit odd, an outsider striding the borderline between sanity and madness, lost in the cyber-house at century's end, obsessed with old age, solitude, mothballs, and the meaning of love.

JOB'S LAMENT

When you finally realize that old age is here to stay, that's when you start cramming your brain with lines
you promised yourself you'd memorize but never got around to doing it. It's an excellent mental exercise.
There are so many passages worth memorizing from Dante, Leopardi, Shakespeare. But right now, Job's
lament is a text I'm particularly fond of:

> They change the night into day;
> The light is short because of darkness.
> If I wait, the grave is mine house;
> I have made my bed in the darkness of the studios.
> I have said to corruption, "Thou art my producer."
> To the worm, "Thou art my actor, and my actress."
> And where is now my hope?

JUDGING A WORK OF ART

Leo Stein admitted purchasing Matisse's Woman in a Hat *because he'd never seen anything so badly painted. Do
you think art attacks by its sheer originality?* ¶ The unique aesthetic criterion I approve of for judging a work
of art is not to ask, rather foolishly, is it ugly? Is it beautiful? Is it original according to certain critical
parameters, various aesthetic theories or the latest post-structuralist theories? All I want to know is: Is it

Juliet (Giulietta Masina) preparing to commit
adultery. (*Juliet of the Spirits*, 1965)

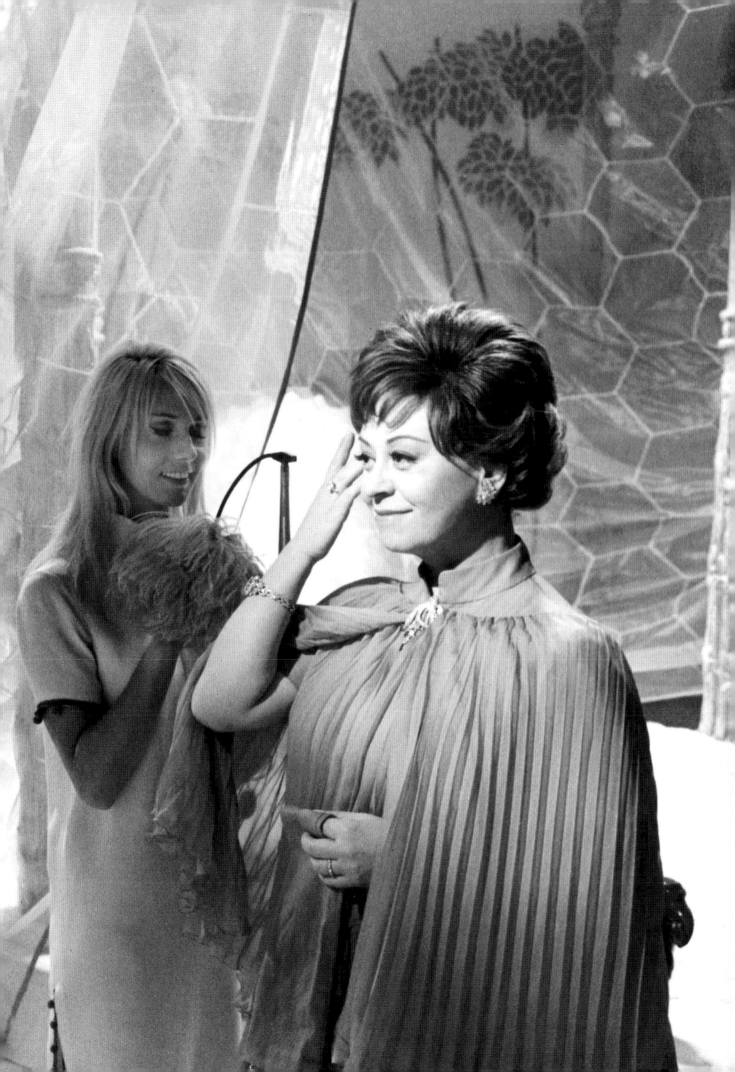

Hallucinatory images of female mental projections. (*Juliet of the Spirits*, 1965)

vital? I can't conceive of anything purer for judging a work of art or for entering into contact with an artis-
ic expression. If the work is vital, then it will possess a mysterious life of its own.

ULIET OF THE SPIRITS

For *Juliet of the Spirits*, I wanted Giulietta [Masina] to play someone on the frontier of magnetic dimensions who finds it hard coming to terms with various levels of reality. In real life, Giulietta has always
seemed to me as someone very down-to-earth and childlike, as opposed to childish. I felt that inventing a
character called Giulietta whose confrontation between her innocent and practical nature and a harsh,
unforgiving reality could result in a series of fantastic mental projections that would destabilize her for a
time but that she'd be capable of mastering in the end. And so the film narrates this struggle that changes
her into a mature and independent woman, possessing the wisdom of a second innocence based on experience. ¶ I will admit that I made a big mistake. The mistake I made was in casting my wife as a simple
housewife, totally dependent on her husband. I should have made her a *celebrated actress* totally dependent
on her husband and trapped in the multiple role of wife, mistress, lover, and friend. The possibilities
would have been richer and more stimulating, the results closer to what I had tried to do in *8 ½*. I don't
recall ever bickering more with Giulietta than during the production of this film. She kept repeating to me
hat she didn't feel comfortable in her role and I just kept telling her to be herself. It never dawned on me
hat "herself" was wife and actress—the key to this film. How could I have been so stubborn? And so the
moral of the story is: never try to second-guess your wife.... Still, it's a good film don't you think?

Powerful images of psychic blockage influenced in part by Fellini's memories of Nazi-occupied Rome. (*Juliet of the Spirits*, 1965)

JUNG

I am terribly impatient with people who dismiss Jung as a nutcase who took himself for an Aryan Christ. People who say that are either in bad faith or totally ignorant of his writings. ¶ What I appreciated in Jung was his championing of the West's return to feeling or intuition, to a widening of consciousness beyond the strict confines of intellect, the necessity to acknowledge the paradoxicality of life. The opposites must balance one another. ¶ Freud, on the other hand, is the better writer. After *Casanova*, I thought of making a film about Freud by adapting his magisterial study of Leonardo da Vinci, including the contested bits where he saw a vulture inserting its beak into the child Leonardo's mouth. Whether or not you agree with Meyer Schapiro on this point hardly matters: it's Freud's interpretation that suggests much about Freud himself.

Famous actor Alberto Lazzari (matinee idol
Amedeo Nazzari, in background) arrives at
the Kit Kat Club in a scene that prefigures
the via Veneto nightlife of *La Dolce Vita*.
(*The Nights of Cabiria*, 1957)

Echo and Narcissus: Fellini framing a close-up of Claudia (Claudia Cardinale). (8 ½, 1963)

KAFKA

I read *The Metamorphosis* at twenty and was stunned by it. At that time, Rome had a menacing, prewar atmosphere that was magnified at night by the eerie blue street lamps. This blue light fell across our faces, making us look like swimmers in a city that had mysteriously sunk underwater. So, under such circumstances, reading Kafka had a tremendous impression on me. He seemed to me like the poet with a third eye who didn't try to explain the mystery of the world but rather see beyond the chaos of appearances into the living yet stony heart of life. To be an artist today is to go on asking the essential questions after Kafka and with Kafka. I've since read all his work and I think that my films have in some fundamental, perhaps unconscious way, been influenced by him. ¶ *I can see Kafka's sensibility in your work, but his vision of life seems much darker than yours.* ¶ Critics claim that my reading *Ulysses* influenced 8 ½. I'd be delighted to acknowledge Joyce but at that point I hadn't read anything by him. It seems to me more pertinent to see an echo of Kafka's influence somewhere at work in the film. In Kafka, there's a mixture of buffoonery and sheer terror that you associate with dreams when you see someone staring at you, laughing silently. In turn, you begin laughing but you have the strangest sensation that your laughter doesn't exist. Then you wake up and there's no rational explanation for it. Your conscience, however, has registered a subconscious situation composed of dramatic, irreducible contrasts so greatly exaggerated that they seem utterly ridiculous. Kafka translates this vision by narrating its incomprehensibility as the purest form of truth.

KILL YOUR DARLINGS

For a filmmaker, self-indulgence is a difficult trap to avoid. Faulkner's injunction to "kill your darlings" is sound advice and great artists like Bergman and Kurosawa have honed it to perfection. However, killing my darlings can only spell disaster for someone like me.

Fellini with Giulietta Masina (Cabiria), Oscar D'Onofrio (François Périer), and assistant director Dominique Delouche (sunglasses) on location at Castel Gandolfo, south of Rome. (*The Nights of Cabiria*, 1957)

KUROSAWA, BERGMAN, AND BUÑUEL

Rashomon was the first film I saw by Kurosawa. I remember how I remained absolutely enchanted by this film, above and beyond the story itself, which I saw in Japanese and which enhanced its charm even more because it's a language totally foreign to me. Seeing it in the original version gave the characters a striking allure of mystery because you never understood if they were expressing joy or rage, if they wanted to kiss or to skewer one another with a sword. *Rashomon* revealed to me a great Japanese master who had succeeded in photographing not only the air itself but through it and beyond. For example, he shows us the woodcutter walking through the forest, an axe over his shoulder while sunlight is continuously thrown from the blade onto the shimmering leaves. It's an example of how filmmaking can express the reality around us in the most fantastic and complex ways. ¶ Ingmar Bergman achieved this in *Wild Strawberries* using a darker, more lugubrious vision of reality that was pathological, painfully intimate, and influenced by psychoanalysis. But he succeeded, above all, in *The Face*, which I adored. It's the story of a wandering medium, an ambulatory actor, a bohemian with magical powers. Bergman tries to show, in a more spectral manner than Kurosawa, the possibility of the coexistence of other dimensions and the riches of the human psyche. ¶ Buñuel is the *auteur* I feel closest to in terms of an idea of cinema or the tendency to make particular kinds of films. Buñuel had an inimitable approach to cinema because he was capable of capturing the impalpability, the ineffability of dreams. In contrast to Bergman, Buñuel offers the kind of cinema that dreams in our place. *El*—what a masterpiece! A film that made a great impression on me at a time when I needed to believe that movies could attempt other things than filming a shabby man on a bicycle.

OPPOSITE: Temptations of the damned: con artist Augusto Rocca (Broderick Crawford) at a wild party put on by his gangster friends. (*The Swindle*, 1955) ABOVE: Brute force: Anthony Quinn as traveling strongman Zampanò. (*La Strada*, 1954)

LANGUAGE AND REALITY

I think we constantly live a contradiction where words mask reality more than they reveal it, like a lighthouse enveloped in fog. Words infect reality. Images are made with light and though they pass through dirty spaces, they remain pure. After all, what Moses heard pouring forth from the Burning Bush wasn't the voice of Cecile B. De Mille: it was the fire, God's presence that spoke. You come close to that "presence of the Word" in the medium of film. Tarkovsky's work—or Bergman's—is a good example. Transforming reality into fiction is perhaps simply another of the many amusing ways of deceiving oneself, but I think you can go beyond words in film. My interest in dreams is due, in part, to their concentration on images independent of words.

LA STRADA

Tullio Pinelli wrote, for all intents and purposes, the script of *La Strada*. We'd conceived the subject at the same time, in a kind of orgiastic synchronicity. I was directing *I Vitelloni* and Tullio had gone to see his family in Turin. At that time, there was no *autostrada* between Rome and the north and so you had to drive through the mountains. Along one of the tortuous winding roads, he saw a man pulling a *carretta*, a sort of cart covered in tarpaulin with a roughly sketched mermaid painted onto it. A tiny woman was pushing the cart from behind. When he returned to Rome, he told me what he'd seen and his desire to narrate their hard lives on the road. "It would make the ideal scenario for your next film," he said. It was the same story I'd imagined but with a crucial difference: mine focused on a little traveling circus with a slow-witted

Spaces to fill up, worlds to create: painting a universe in Teatro 5 at Cinecittà. (*Intervista*, 1987)

young woman named Gelsomina. So we merged my flea-bitten circus characters with his smoky campfire mountain vagabonds. Inspired, we named Zampanò, the brutal male protagonist, after the owners of two small circuses in Rome: Zamperla and Saltano.

LIFE

Transience, I always say, is a permanent part of the human condition. We're just tourists in the land called Life.

LOOKING GOOD

Last weekend, Guilietta and I were invited to a fancy reception and she complained of my looking shabby. "There are holes in your tuxedo," she whispered to me, mortified. "You ought to be impressed," I told her. "We've got an aristocratic moth in the house: it only eats holes in full dress suits."

LSD

You used LSD in a controlled experiment supervised by a medical team. Did this adventure provide you with any liberating visions? ❡ No. I remember very little of what went on. On the other hand, my scientific colleagues told me that I spoke for hours on end, pacing nonstop around the room. According to them, my natural condition is to be constantly in motion—but I already knew I was a vagabond, fascinated by clowns and acrobats, by outsiders like me with no permanent address. So here was proof. ❡ *There exists BBC*

Putting ideas to the test: Fellini in the basket leading up to Susy's tree house hideaway. (*Juliet of the Spirits*, 1965)

footage of you in 1965 discussing your LSD experience with Ian Dallas, who played the magician in 8 ½. In that television interview, you describe the "trip" as a deeply subjugating one. ¶ Yes, it was just after the success of *8 ½*; I was drunk on the preparations for *Juliet of the Spirits*, traveling the whole of Italy in search of miraculous encounters, there wasn't a cloud in my sky. To give such a gushingly frank interview, I must have been in one of my euphoric, manic phases. My God, how do I look in that footage? A little crazy, no? ¶ *You look great. You're trim and fit. You've got a wild mane of black hair.* ¶ Ah, good.... The experience was naturally a vision of Heaven and Hell, in keeping with my Catholic upbringing, and like all genuine visions, very difficult to express in words. The long wordless scenes in *Toby Dammit* are the closest I came to expressing what was beyond expression in my experience with LSD. Objects and their functions no longer had any significance. All I perceived was perception itself, the hell of forms and figures devoid of human emotion and detached from the reality of my unreal environment. I was an instrument in a virtual world that constantly renewed its own meaningless image in a living world that was itself perceived outside of nature. And since the appearance of things was no longer definitive but limitless, this paradisiacal awareness freed me from the reality external to my self. The fire and the rose, as it were, became one.

Fellini on the beach at Passo Oscuro with Oscar-winning designer Piero Gherardi's monster fish. (*La Dolce Vita*, 1959)

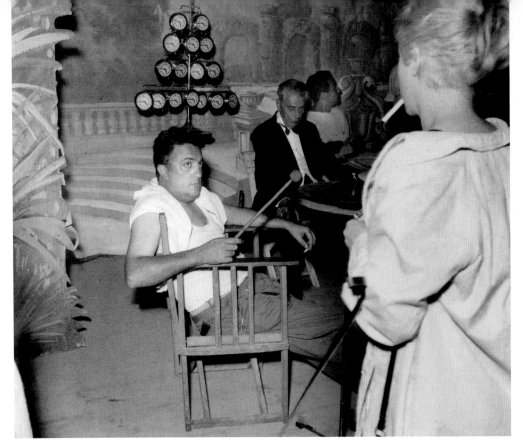

Fellini during a break in shooting the variety theater sequence where Cabiria (Guilietta Masina, right) is hypnotized by The Magician (Aldo Silvani). (*The Nights of Cabiria*, 1957)

MAGIC AND METACINEMA

What can one say about magic? You'd like to see me rise in my chair and float around the room? That I direct films based on the phenomenon of levitation? ¶ *Levitation, transmigration, astrology...* ¶ No, no, I don't want to frighten you! During the preparations for *Juliet of the Spirits*, I was introduced to a monk who claimed to levitate from his seat in the front pew to alight on the altar like Joseph of Copertino—and he proved it by flying onto the altar. Another transformed himself into a horse—I actually saw the poor man's head elongate into a horse's long rectangular skull with black bulging eyes and snorting nostrils. He possessed some kind of optical power to make you think you saw this. And then there was the apparition of Casanova called up by my good friend Gustavo Rol, the celebrated magus. I badly needed advice on my film about the Latin lover, and his apparition provided nothing but worthless idiocies. Or the time I transgressed Rol's strict rules and fell sick, unable to eat or sleep for two days running. ¶ *What had you transgressed exactly?* ¶ The seven of clubs. Rol was demonstrating a card trick. I had to pick a card at random from the pack and came up with the seven of clubs. With his customary solemnity, Rol told me to keep it flat against my chest without looking at it. He then asked me, "Into which card should I transform it?" So I picked another card at random. "Into the ten of hearts," I replied. ¶ But he warned me: "Remember, Federico. Do not, at any time, look at the seven of clubs." ¶ With the card pressed against my chest, Rol began investing my hand and the seven of clubs with his fierce, penetrating gaze. Unfortunately, I was seized with an irresistible urge to look at the card. I have never forgotten what I saw: a grisly, grayish putrefying mess, a mush of stinking porridge in which the contours of the seven of clubs slowly dissolved and ran

Stars are born: Anita Ekberg and Marcello Mastroianni during a break in the mammoth production. (*La Dolce Vita*, 1959)

down the card, leaving a bloody lace of spidery veins. At that moment, what seemed like a hand grasped my intestines and wrenched them violently. Before I passed out, however, I had the satisfaction of holding the ten of hearts in my hand. ¶ I'm reporting the facts as I witnessed them. ¶ I am curious. Everything interests me and I believe in all of it. This seems to me the sanest, healthiest way of accommodating the irrational. And anyway, how could I be cynical, overcautious, and skeptical, with the line of work I'm in? I make a living in a high-risk industry that never ceases to prove I'm out of my mind! I dream, I imagine something, and then pull it out of my hat in front of millions of people. Call it what you like but for me that's magic. I ask you, how is that possible? How is it possible that I, for the most part ignorant of politics, philosophy, or some other protective ideology, lacking an overwhelming passion—I've remained an adolescent filled with wonder and curiosity—how is it that I could have accomplished what it takes to make a film? I'm not talking about aesthetic results but rather the operation itself. It all seems beyond me. So how can I not believe in magic? ¶ *Would this help explain why your films are often self-reflexive, metacinematic?* ¶ In part. I'm genuinely awestruck by what my technicians are capable of doing, by the very nature of the medium, by the phenomenon of light recorded on a photographic plate, to the extent that I want simply to stand back and film what I'm filming, rejoicing in this hall of mirrors that the studio has become.

MARCELLO MASTROIANNI

The three things I treasure about working with Marcello is that he never asks to read the script, he never analyzes his role, and he never questions the hidden meanings of a scene. It's as if he's totally present yet

M

Metacinematic illusions: Marcello Mastroianni as Mandrake the Magician. (*Intervista*, 1987)

entirely absent at one and the same time. This is his great quality as an actor. Doing exactly what I tell him to do the instant I need him to do it keeps his *jeu d'acteur* fresh, spontaneous, ensuring a kind of perpetual happening on the set. Another marvelous quality is his capacity to listen. Patiently, like a schoolboy chum or a partner in crime, Marcello has listened to me for hours expounding on characters and situations that later became material for new films. ¶ After *La Dolce Vita*, Marcello was swamped with enticing offers, especially from Hollywood, but these he turned down. He was afraid of being typecast. "An actor," he said, "is a banderol that waves in the wind by his own breath. He mustn't always blow on the same side otherwise he becomes a ship that rapidly reaches America. If you're a cowboy and the public like you, you're a cowboy until you're president." ¶ The only time we ever clashed was during the shooting of *8 ½* when I asked him to shave the hair on his chest. Shocked, he refused outright, complaining that it was unseemly for an Italian male. I explained to him that Guido must be perceived as an immature forty-three year old, incapable of organizing his complex inner world, a big baby with diaper rash. The hairy torso had to go. We fought and argued until finally I told him, "Listen, Marcellino, if you lose your sense of humor we'll never make a comic film." ¶ He shaved.

MASTORNA

The *Voyage of G. Mastorna* is a project, an idea, a fantasy that I conceived and wrote after *Juliet of the Spirits* and that has had a genesis plagued by opposition, various obstacles and that, at some point, was steeped in a vaguely superstitious atmosphere. It's a project that has punctually presented itself to me at the end of

A wary Encolpio (Martin Potter) advancing through the wasteland constructed at Cinecittà. (*Fellini's Satyricon*, 1969)

every film I've made since *Juliet*, almost with the will to say, "This time, it's my turn. This time, you direct me." I've always turned it away and will continue to do so. The story itself hasn't influenced me really because it's remained intact in all its episodes, but its atmosphere undoubtedly has because atmosphere is always the most intimate and secret part of a story. And so *Mastorna* has nourished, impregnated, all my films since 1965. There's a little of *Mastorna* in the *Satyricon*, in *City of Women*, and even in *Casanova*. *Mastorna* is like a sunken ship that continues to emit from the abyss a radioactivity that, without diminishing in any way its own integrity as a story or an idea, has supplied, will go on supplying, all my future films. But it's true that at one point, I really thought *Mastorna* was jinxed. I asked Dino Buzatti to work on it in 1965, I think. Dino developed a tumor and died a few years later. I continued scripting the film until I contracted Sanarelli-Schwarzmann Syndrome—you really have to have a hex on you to come down with something like that—and almost died. Then, I began working on it with Tonino Guerra, who'd written *And the Ship Sails On* with me, and *Blow Up* for Antonioni. He developed cancer of the gums and had to bow out. So I put *Mastorna* on the shelf until recently: I'm toying around with the idea of making it into a comic strip. ¶ For me, there's no dividing line between reality and imagination. It's true that *Mastorna* is about life after death, but my hero has lost something insignificant to others but of great emotional importance to him. He manages to enter the labyrinth of his memory containing countless exits but only one entrance.... I haven't found that entrance yet. I can't say any more about the film. It continues to elude me, but I pretend that one day I'll direct it.

Directing an orgy scene with a wanton hunchback
(Angelica Hansen), a worn out Casanova (Donald
Sutherland), and buxom Astrodi (Marika Rivera).
(*Fellini's Casanova*, 1976)

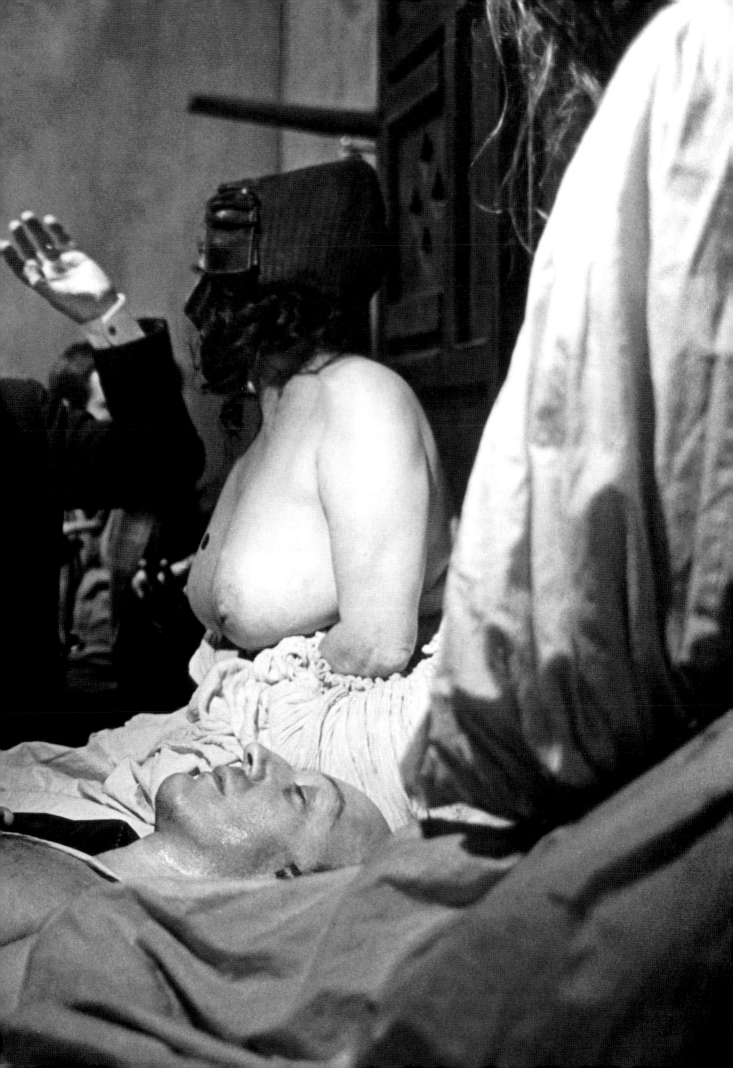

Directing Anna Magnani, the Maestro's symbol of Rome. (*Fellini's Roma*, 1972)

MEDIUM-ARTISAN

Do you have a particular process that consists of turning a real person into a felliniesque character? ¶ I don't have a particular system that I practice religiously. I'm faithful to one thing only: the principle of being receptive by placing myself wholly at the service of the fantasies I want to materialize. I never make the mistake of adapting the actor to a character: I tailor the role to the individual. Every film is different from the next and every moment different from every other. So I don't have a system. I couldn't establish a film school. My sole guide is receptivity, open-mindedness. What is an artist, after all? A medium. In a way, he's only a mind, a network of nerves, a body, hands: a simulacrum destined to be inhabited by a kind of dream, a fantasy, an idea, which then becomes characters and situations, a story. An artist's imperative is to succeed in materializing his story through experience and craftsmanship. A medium-artisan.

MEMORY

We need to distinguish between recollection and memory. There are two kinds of memory, one Proustian, the other Platonic. Recollection or the remembrance of things past is banal: events can be recalled or they can be invented, as I've done in the majority of my films. Memory, on the other hand, is like the soul: it lives before birth. Take Plato's *Phaedo* and the slave boy, for exámple. Socrates demonstrates that the untaught child knows Euclid and Pythagoras. In that sense, I too was a slave boy: my Socrates was Rossellini and what I knew intuitively was cinema. Child Federico is father to the man. Memory doesn't express itself through recollection. It's a mysterious indefinable component urging us to enter into con-

Fellini in a playful mood with Janet Suzman (Edmea Tetua). (*And the Ship Sails On*, 1983)

tact with dimensions, events, sensations we can't name but that we know, however confusedly, existed before us. Forgive me this rather pompous definition but an artist lives in his memory, constantly remembering people, places, and situations that never have existed in the context of his life. The obligation to express is focused on the invention of memories. Perhaps I'm contradicting my previous statements on the subject—including the critics who insist that my films are born and breast-fed on my own memories—but I don't have a memory made up of personal recollections. It's simply more natural for me to invent my own, inspired by the memory of lives and events that never existed but which feeds on them or calls them into existence. I invented everything, including my birth. And this invented self is the only true self I see reflected in the mirror of my films. I invented my youth, my family, relationships with women and with life. I have always invented. The irrepressible urge to invent is because I don't want anything autobiographical in my films. I invented Guido Anselmi and the critics declared he's me. But Guido is not my alter ego just as I'm not Mastroianni. That would be too simple. In *City of Women*, he's my Snàporaz, a representation of myself in a certain sense, but I'm also the role played by Ettore Manni. In *Ginger and Fred*, I'm Marcello and Giulietta, the TV presenter, and the dwarfs as well. Making yourself up is an offshoot of our modernity. So I'm everything and nothing. I am what I invent.

THE MICHELANGELO PROJECT

A project based on the life of Michelangelo was proposed to me by the American television station CBS or NBC—I can't remember which—around the same time that I was to make a film of Dante's *Divine Comedy*,

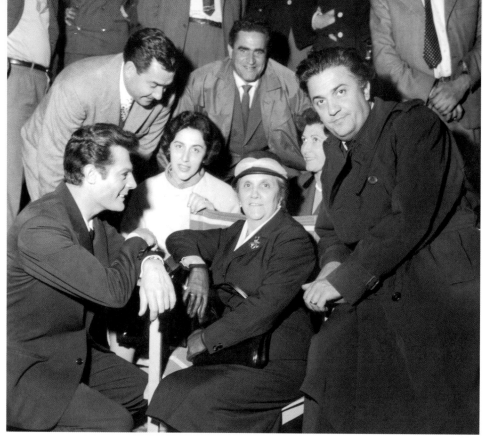

Marcello Mastroianni with Fellini and his mother, Ida Barbiani (seated), on location near the Trevi Fountain. (*La Dolce Vita*, 1959)

"The film wasn't up to much," explained the producer, "but for this remake we hope the book's dialogue will inspire you." I'd seen the film based on Irving Stone's famous novel and thought there was room for improvement, so I thought I'd read the book. I still remember bits of that "terrific dialogue":

> *"Have you ever been in love?"*
> *"In a way."*
> *"It's always 'in a way.'"*
> *"The way the people on Vesuvius forgot to run from the lava: it had covered them before they knew*
>   *it was coming."*
> *"What fell on your nose, Michelangelo?"*
> *"A ham."*
> *"From a butcher's rack? Did you forget to duck?"*

It wasn't difficult refusing the project.

MOM AND DAD

I've invented several bohemian stories: being born on a train from Naples to Rome, fleeing a suffocating family atmosphere to join a circus, making love to my nanny, and so on, but none of it's true. What is true was the impact of the Catholic Church on our family life: omnipresent and stifling, so much so, in fact,

Broderick Crawford as Augusto Rocca, the *bidonista*, or confidence man, who swindles his victims while posing as a priest. (*The Swindle*, 1955)

that my mother insisted on my becoming a cardinal. But I never could have been happy as a man of the cloth. There's a very strong tradition in Italian society that one of the sons of a noble family, but not exclusively noble, enter the priesthood, or that a daughter become a nun. This is part of the history of Italian families who saw, in this way, a means of gaining access to the power and protection of the Church. However, my family wasn't especially noble and perhaps that explains why I managed to escape my destiny as a priest. Dad was a traveling salesman. Mom a Barbiani whose roots ran very deep in Roman society. They met and fell in love at the Pantanella pasta factory on the outskirts of Rome. He was a good-looking gentleman with a devastating smile and she eloped with him, despite her family's vehement protests. Unfortunately, they weren't at all suited for each other and it seems to me that Mom cried ever afterward. Dad was the absent husband and father, much loved and sorely missed, forever on the run. "I am what I am," he would tell her. "Nature imagined me." Or something grand like that.

MUSIC

Music for my films usually began with my humming a little tune in a noisy café with friends. If I liked the snippet, and when Nino [Rota] was part of this world, I would call him to arrange a meeting. I'd sit down at the piano beside him and hum my vague and meager musical tune. He'd pick it up and run with it until the phrase became a melody. I enjoyed working this way and often, even before I had an idea for a film, the melodies Nino invented would stimulate characters and situations for new projects. When enough music was written and recorded, I had it played during rehearsals and his music became a living part of

Metaphors of artistic paralysis: the infernal traffic jam that swallows up Fellini's crew on a Cinecittà back lot. (*Fellini's Roma*, 1972)

In the footsteps of Georges Meliès and the pioneers of cinema: fabricating the illusion of a moving carriage. (*Fellini's Casanova*, 1976)

the film, as important as lighting, faces, decors, and dialogue. On the other hand, I always avoid listening to music at home. Great music fills me with remorse. Music has a domino effect on me. It's a kind of insidious cruelty that creeps up on you while it plays, reminding you that plenitude, peace, and harmony are within your grasp, and then all at once it's over; you've been living a pipe dream for the past half-hour precisely because you don't have plenitude or peace or harmony. And then, because it's over, the feeling of nostalgia sets in, that forgotten country of remembered things. So now you're adrift in a sea of sadness asking yourself why the hell the music died....No, life is a carnival to be lived in the present, not a concert hall where you're dragged down continuously into the past.

MY TRUE HOME
I wake up early, around six o'clock. I get up, try and do some exercises—I try and then give up. I walk around the house, open and shut windows, make coffee, telephone friends. Then I go out and take the production company car waiting near the house. I get in and invite the driver to take the longest route possible because it's during this drive, during this little half-hour, that I try and gather my thoughts about what I'm going to film. While we're crossing the city, it seems to me that all this bustle and movement—the people, trams, cars, city life starting up again—help me, force me almost, to realize that I have to go to work. The privilege of having a chauffeur-driven car and the sight of thousands of people rushing off to work make me feel guilty because, honestly, I don't know what I'm going to do when I get to the studio. Like a good Catholic, the sense of culpability forces me to organize my thoughts, to anticipate what my

morning might hold. But working like this can't be defined as improvisation because it's the state of mind necessary for confronting a day's work in the studio. And then, once I'm in the studios, I've reached my true home, the place I've always lived in. The troupe, the lights, the costumes, all of it is so familiar, so indispensable to me. ¶ *Would you say that your emotional state has a direct influence on your work?* ¶ During the winter, I may arrive at the studios with a bad cold, but even if I'm running a temperature, the cold and fever will disappear. I warn my assistants, who panic and phone the doctor so as to reassure the producer that work won't be interrupted, and I have to insist that all the fuss is unnecessary since, in a few minutes, I'll be perfectly well if left alone. It's the atmosphere in the studio and the kind of work I do, the people I work with—actors, makeup artists, gaffers, grips, cameramen—all of it is profoundly therapeutic for me. In a half-hour, a fever of 38 degrees [100.4 degrees Fahrenheit] will disappear and I can begin working. It's subconscious yoga—finding oneself in the right place at the right time—and all is well. However, it's not the kind of therapeutic advice I'd want to share with everyone who's caught the flu: Come to Cinecittà! Soak your feet on the set and you'll be cured! That would be very costly treatment when two aspirins is all you need. But even if I can work during an illness, I never allow myself to be influenced by a mood or an emotional state except if it's completely at the service of the game I'm directing.

Shooting the famous ending that won Giulietta
Masina the prize for Best Actress at the Cannes
Film Festival. (*The Nights of Cabiria*, 1957)

ABOVE: Janet Suzman as the diva Edmea Tetua in a film that celebrates a movie-making process doomed to extinction. (*And the Ship Sails On*, 1983) OPPOSITE: Prostitutes on display at a high-class, state-controlled brothel. (*Fellini's Roma*, 1972)

NAPLES AND VENICE

The Japanese are extremely keen on a total conquest of the Occident—from a technical, industrial, and financial standpoint. Sony and two other Japanese companies have founded a film group with the goal of rendering a cinematographic homage to Europe by sponsoring films directed by five European filmmakers and I'm among the five chosen. I think it's intelligent and very shrewd on their part. I'll film portraits of Venice and Naples. With Venice, I would simply show my impressions, the dreams I have of this mysterious, incredible city rotting on stakes, and yet miraculously resistant to the hoards of tourists, pollution, high tides, and floods. A city forever dying. With Naples, I'll deal with her two sides: the *paradiso* and the *inferno* of a city that is a curious blend of wisdom and madness, of the sacred and the profane. Naples is like a human being, really, with extremes of need, arrogant, decadent, ghastly, and sublime, as well as a cauldron of extraordinarily expressive faces. ¶ *Why not a portrait of Milano?* ¶ Because it doesn't inspire me as a city. Milano examines you in a very unpleasant way: Are you a good businessman? Are you capable of making money? Rome, on the other hand, is profoundly maternal, she never forces you to make a living. She's totally indifferent to money, to material success. Rome lets you sleep on her rooftops. And what could be more pleasant than a rooftop? That's been my vocation since childhood. On a rooftop, you can lie down and be content to be nothing.

NARCISSISM

Is narcissism an essential vice for the artist? ¶ Beyond the amusing aspects of creation, the invention of a world, of characters and situations, and the resolution of an incredible number of technical problems, of craftsman-

Fellini with the French actress Magali Noël who plays Fanny, a variety show performer. (*La Dolce Vita*, 1959)

ship, but above all, expression, there exists a more profound, more secret, more impudent satisfaction that has to do with the myth of Narcissus and the idea of an almost quasi-divine power. A creator almost always has an air of God the Father about him, the exception being that we take a little longer than seven days to make a world. So a novelist, a storyteller speaks only about himself. He's obliged, forced to speak only about himself. ¶ *Why forced?* ¶ People think that filmmaking is a 35mm camera and that the reality around us is there to be photographed simply and directly. However, the director *behind* the camera always puts himself in *front* of it. If not, his cinema offers us a contradictory reality. By expressing his private sphere of emotions and dreams, his proper vision of the world—by trying *not* to be objective—an artist is more faithful to reality. So I never had the preoccupation of leaving neorealism behind because I never identified with it in the first place, even if I worked alongside Rossellini. It was a great experience, like so many other things, but I never felt as though it were an aesthetic theory I had to follow.

NEW NARRATIVE TECHNIQUES

Fellini's Roma was a film inspired by my love for the bikini: something that begins nowhere and ends all at once.

NINO ROTA

In *And the Ship Sails On*, I named the ship *Gloria N.* leaving the "N." in suspense because I didn't know what it stood for. I realized later that it meant "Gloria Nino." When he died, I was left with a kingdom of silent shadows.

I Adore Interviews! A self-portrait by Fellini sketched during the filmed interviews.

THE NONEXISTENT INTERVIEW

Is there nothing that terrifies you in the murky depths of your unconscious? ¶ Interviews, in general. ¶ *Interviews…?* ¶ When I was young, I hated passing exams; they gave me nightmares. Now, it's interviews. Journalists and film critics take me to task for granting too many interviews but they're always the first in line to request an exclusive! In actual fact, I grant very few. The reluctance to grant interviews isn't because I want to render myself more mysterious but rather the objective recording of a troubled state of being during the interview process: everything assumes the air of a university examination. ¶ *Well then, let's call these examinations* The Nonexistent Interview, *in homage to Calvino and as a gentle and affectionate form of terrorism.* ¶ *Ecco!* I see you're filming with three cameras: if they're going to be nonexistent, these interviews should be conducted in silence and in the dark. My God, let's reinvent the interview! New! Improved! The Fellini Interview is now high performing, more stimulating to the imagination! ¶ *Excellent idea. We're now plunged in total darkness and silence.* ¶ *Va bene!* I can hear myself think, but it sounds like vague, tedious, insincere fibbing all over again. ¶ *Insincere fibbing?* ¶ Yes, you've got to help me to lie more sincerely. ¶ *Federico, you're in the dark where no one can hear you. Try and be sincere for once.* ¶ But how can I? The interview format creates a slight case of schizophrenia, a dichotomy between how people perceive you and how you perceive yourself. People presume I have an answer to everything when in fact I haven't any confidence in what I'm saying. I don't like sitting on a pedestal. I couldn't tell you if I were a moron or an oxymoron. So I have to make up stories out of fear of disappointing everyone. In the end, however, I'm ready to admit that if I hate interviews I also enjoy them for two simple reasons. *Uno*, they force me to reflect. *Due*, they're a constant challenge—I won't say threat—to my powers of invention.

OBSCURE BEING

Sometimes, when I see my films again by chance—I never deliberately watch them—or when I come across a photo still or an excerpt on television, I immediately ask myself the question, Who made this film? Because it couldn't have been me. How is it possible that I could have imposed my will on these hundreds of people? Could I have really gone that far and outraged the powers that be? I am literally stupefied and so I must imagine that I am someone else. The moment I begin working, the instant I become a filmmaker, I'm inhabited by an obscure being unknown to me who takes command of the ship, directing everything in my place. I offer my voice to him, my sense of craftsmanship, my strategies of persuasion and seduction, plagiarism, and tyranny. But it's someone else who reacts, another with whom I live and whom I partially come to know because I hear friends talking about him. On reading the critics, sometimes I discover the truth about my obscure Other.

ORATORS

Having had to endure the likes of Mussolini, my generation is very suspicious of orators: all that oral stimulation going on in public places, especially to orgasm.

ORCHESTRA REHEARSAL

It's curious the number of people who have attacked me for making *Orchestra Rehearsal*, claiming that it's an apology for Fascism. The mind boggles! Others insisted that since I'd finally taken an interest in politics and that the film is my first political essay, I ought to be forgiven my naivety. Still others criticized the film as being reactionary, conservative, or else a hodgepodge of mystical assertions, a political allegory. *Orchestra Rehearsal* is none of those things: it's an ethical apologue that takes its cue from "The Orchestral Conductor" in Elias Canetti's *Crowds and Power*, a monumental reflection on the nature of violence, a classic that my learned friend Brunello Rondi suggested I read during the making of *Casanova*: "Thus for the orchestra the conductor literally embodies the work they are playing, the simultaneity of the sounds as well as their sequence; and since, during the performance, nothing is supposed to exist except this work, for so long is the conductor the ruler of the world." I actually toyed with the idea of using this quotation in the opening credits but thought better of it. It's not my style.

ORIGINS OF A FILM

A film, even if it's very complex to direct and demands a lot of time, can exist in a sensation, a suspicion, in anticipation or a kind of second sight. It could be a flash of light, a sound, a woman's perfume, or the tremor of a leaf that contains the entire universe…. One says so many things, but I think it's true despite the romantic claptrap. An entire life can be suggested by the idea of a creature struggling to be born.

Ecclesiastical fashion parade: Fellini's
satirical vision of the Catholic Church.
(*Fellini's Roma*, 1972)

Suffocating images of a red velvet clergy. (*Fellini's Roma*, 1972)

PAINTERS

As a child, I never felt that I was singled out for something special, that I had a particular calling. If I did, I don't remember being aware of it. I had a very confused idea of what I wanted to be and I felt uncomfortable because all my classmates had clear ideas about their future careers. One had decided to become an admiral and he achieved exactly that. I was the least certain of all. I only knew what I didn't want to do with my life. I knew for certain that I wasn't going to be a lawyer like my father wanted nor a cardinal as my mother hoped. I really let her down…. ¶ I was attracted to certain people who were considered, here in Italy, as extravagant, eccentric, marginal individuals to be frowned on: painters. I was fascinated by them because they wore their hair long, washed little, had dirty fingernails, dressed in the gaudiest colors, the most outrageous costumes, appeared caked with paint in the company of beautiful women, ate whatever and whenever they liked—usually in their studios—and I admired them because they were classed as vagabonds. It wasn't so much that I wanted to be a painter: I was drawn to their rebellious lifestyle. A child is naturally rebellious being constrained by rules imposed at home and at school, by taboos. My generation was crucified with taboos fostered by the Catholic Church and by Fascism. So a painter, in his way of dressing, his lack of a nine-to-five job, became an image of freedom. I thought to myself: I can't paint, I can't sculpt, but this way of life is imprinted in my genes.

PANTHEON

2001 is fast approaching. Are you planning something to celebrate? ¶ Well, it is a date…. What do you think I should do? ¶ *Why not shoot a film inside the Pantheon? Have you never thought of filming inside that*

Giulietta Masina and Richard Basehart in his role as the swindler Picasso on location near Monte Marino. (*The Swindle*, 1955)

felliniesque space? ¶ No, but I have thought of reconstructing it in Studio 5. Imagine the scene: an immense, tenebrous, utterly void cavity lit by a lamp suspended from its Piranesi dome, with dark green walls dripping of slime, where a menacing, eerie silence reigns supreme. At the stroke of midnight, on the nanosecond of the year 2001, I destroy the Pantheon with a mighty earthquake! What better way to end this appalling century?

PASOLINI

Pasolini's novel, *Ragazzi di vita*, was a scandalous and resounding success. Naturally I fell in love with the text, its expressive limpid style, the courageous, accurate description of Rome's street kids—so much so in fact that I invented the story of a band of homeless children who squat an entire tenement building on the outskirts of Rome and the strange, virtually telepathic communication that goes on between them. It was a film influenced by Pasolini's novel and Buñuel's *Los Olvidados* and another of my thousand and one shelved projects. At any rate, I wanted to meet Pier Paolo and called him. We arranged to meet at Canova's. I arrived early and when he appeared in the doorway, I saw the taut and dusty body of a bantam boxer—not at all the ascetic poet I'd imagined in Marxist terms. He walked over to my table with a curious elastic stride as if his short legs had springs, removed his sunglasses and timidly, without pretension, introduced himself. We immediately struck up a friendship—it was impossible not to like him: he possessed such a rich, spontaneous, and generous temperament. That very afternoon and for weeks afterward, we went to see films together. I learned a great deal from his sharp, inspired commentary that he usually made in a hushed whisper while the film was running

Self-reliant prostitute Cabiria Ceccarelli (Giulietta Masina) practicing her trade on the Passeggiata Archeologica. (*The Nights of Cabiria*, 1957)

and it was clear, even then, that he wanted to direct. Later on, I invited him to collaborate on the dialogue for *Nights of Cabiria* because his ear for the slang of Rome's low-life characters was unmatched by anyone writing in films at that time. I had asked for a contribution of about ten pages: he turned in forty. I used only a handful of the slang expressions, worried that this ingenious and sordid, highly eroticized gutter language would have the Catholic censors in an uproar. The film, moreover, would have taken on a much darker, sinister air than the tragicomic tone I was after. On the set, however, watching the making of *Cabiria*, Pier Paolo grew more and more interested in the art of directing. After the international success of *La Dolce Vita*, I had set up a production company called Federiz—after Federico and Angelo Rizzoli, the producer of *La Dolce Vita*. The goal was to share my success with the best young talents in Italy by producing their work and one day, Pier Paolo came to me with his script, *Accatone*. It was a brilliant script, of course, and I showed it to Rizzoli. That's when things went bad. Rizzoli had no patience with homosexuals and, in particular, homosexual communists. Still, my enthusiasm and authority managed to convince both Rizzoli and Clemente Fracassi, my eternally pessimistic partner in charge of finances, to fund a small crew that would allow Pier Paolo to shoot some screen tests. Unfortunately, the tests were less than satisfactory. It was a simple case of bad luck on Pasolini's part. His great love of cinema, of Carl Dreyer, and his proven talent for narration should have produced excellent material. Under extreme pressure, however, his natural timidity botched the screen tests and consequently, his debut under my supervision. In retrospect, I should have stood up to Clemente and Rizzoli, but in truth I was already weary with the constant battles going on at Federiz, the sheer lack of audaciousness and in due course, when the company folded, I felt nothing but relief.

Shooting the dawn sequence after the orgy on the beach at Passo Oscuro. (*La Dolce Vita*, 1959)

PICASSO

Picasso is like a wellspring. He is so great a creator that it seems to me he inhabits the oneiric imagination of artists as the archetype of all that's nourishing. Once, during a period of deep depression, at the start of *8½*, which I no longer wanted to do, I dreamt that Picasso invited me to his modest cabin in the country. He welcomed me warmly and prepared an omelet with twelve eggs he had gathered himself. He motioned for me to sit down at his table and I shyly accepted. He gave me a cloth napkin saying, "Never make stains." I remember that, while we sat there sharing the omelet—which was delicious—Picasso talked to me the whole night as though to an old and very dear friend. I woke up refreshed. ¶ But once again, weeks later, I was deeply depressed and dreamed of Picasso but this time he didn't make us an omelet! We were swimming in the sea and he had his back to me. I wanted to turn around and head for shore because the sky had grown overcast and the waves had started to swell. I realized how far out we were and when I lost sight of Picasso I panicked. Suddenly, I saw a face emerge from the boiling, menacing waves. It was Picasso's bald head with its monk's crown of white hair, his brown robust shoulders and powerful arms swimming, swimming, and cutting the leaden-colored waves in sharp, powerful strokes. I shouted, "I want to turn back!" and Picasso just shook his head and said, "No! No!" and urged me to go on. But I was exhausted and starting sinking. ¶ These dreams show how the figure of Picasso as supreme artist gave me the strength and the guidance I needed during a very difficult period of my life. Another marvelous "chaser-of-doubts" was Georges Simenon. He's appeared in situations similar to those of Picasso but instead of an omelet, he'd offer me a variety of French cheeses. My heart goes out to all those figures that have

P

Fellini with his director of photography
Giuseppe Rotunno on a set designed by
Danilo Donati. (*Fellini's Satyricon*, 1969)

Grand opera: an oddball aristocrat on a ship of fools. (*And the Ship Sails On*, 1983)

appeared to me in the night, in key dreams during moments of artistic doubt and failure. ¶ *What about Picasso as an influence on filmic narration?* ¶ While filming *La Dolce Vita*, I had the idea of taking a statue, breaking it, and then recomposing the pieces in his cubist style. I wanted to do something other than narrate a story in the same old way, like a nineteenth-century novel, although I'm not condemning traditional narrative structures. I repeat, Picasso is an irradiating source. I remember dedicating one of my innumerable drawings of Anita Ekberg to Picasso. ¶ *There is the commonplace that suffering and the lack of financial security are indispensable to the artist. What's the most propitious atmosphere for an artist, in your view?* ¶ When he's obliged to work, period. Picasso hammered away a lifetime at his art. And so it is with me. It doesn't seem that things have changed much from my childhood when I scribbled with crayons. Or the days when I was so enthusiastic about puppets and the miniature theater my parents gave me for my birthday. Or the time I first began drawing comic sketches for newspapers in Florence and Milan. Or when I wrote gags and scripts for radio.... There really hasn't been a great diversity. Perhaps I've acquired a little more technique, my sense of craftsmanship has evolved. Picasso, until the few minutes preceding his death, showed proof of continued research and originality. He took risks right up until the end. I have always made the films I wanted to make and will go on doing so. I have never compromised to make a film.

POETS

Money is everywhere but so is poetry. What we lack are the poets. Producers assume they're poets, of course, because they think they have a public. I do what I do because it's the only thing I know. It seems

Clowns of war: the Grand Duke of Herzog (Fiorenzo Serra). (*And the Ship Sails On*, 1983)

that I was made, more or less painfully, more or less happily, to be a film director. Real life doesn't interest me.

POLITICS

I am more left of center than Dante and a little more to the right than [Ludovico] Ariosto.

PREDESTINATION

How can anyone seriously explain predestination—the merging of the quotidian with destiny? I'm an intuitive—not a philosopher—and what I'm about to say will sound ridiculous but I'll say it anyway: predestination is better understood if we place the catalyst of anguish somewhere on a more mysterious level. I think that what we call chance or wisdom or religious feeling is the ability to coincide one's normal existence with that of a predetermined existence, a kind of "sur-existence" running parallel to daily life and one that is rarely perceptible or understood. Poets write of those moments of rare intensity when the veils part and the baroque architectural design reveals itself behind the baked mud huts of our lives. I lack the incisive logic that would make this declaration less opaque. But the poverty of these words doesn't mask my faith in the flow of things like the swimmer who dives into a river and heads downstream, surviving the waterfall, avoiding the rocks, resting at regular intervals on the banks of the river, confident he'll eventually reach the sea. So, not for me the life of the salmon! The absurd heroism of heading upstream! The

Fellini on set giving precise directions on how and where to stand. (*Fellini's Casanova*, 1976)

of my work, where everything has to be ordered and defined in advance, willed from unconscious drives. I feel that my whole life has been a single creative act directing one long film in which the protagonist, however cleverly disguised or transformed, is always himself in the end. And since films are my life then it follows that I am a film—a metaphor as ridiculous as my being a train! ¶ Let's say, then, that all the world's a film and I'm an actor playing his little part. My script was conceived at birth and every day I find myself reading my lines. I haven't been miscast nor given a consistently bad performance. I married the right woman for a man like me, met my circle of good friends at the time I needed them. I was extraordinarily lucky not to have gone against these so-called chance encounters, not to have turned down an opportunity or been duped by someone, to have intuitively recognized an individual as the future friend who would be of invaluable help to me and, I trust, reciprocally. I have never underestimated the opportunity of making friends or confiding in them. And yet, there remains the constant fretting and strutting around an all too brief candle. Anguish is like a web to which all things adhere. Without it, our lives would be oversimplified. One thinks, "Well, well. Fellini had it all offered to him. Never worried, never suffered. Can you believe his luck?"

PRODIGALITY

Do you ever reshoot a scene? ¶ Never. I destroy a decor right after the final shot. ¶ *Isn't that terribly expensive?* ¶ It's disastrous! But that's the way I work. I need to maintain links to the subconscious in order to remain faithful to my imagination. ❡ *Doesn't that make you an expensive director to produce?* ❡ My prodigality is legend and totally untrue. It's a lie invented by all those who have an interest in flooding money into my films, the reasons for which are pointless to debate. I consider myself as one of the most economical filmmakers in the business because I know exactly what I want and how to obtain it. A real decor would certainly be cheaper but it wouldn't be part of the cinema I'm interested in. For me, the invented thing is more real than a perfectly reflected reality. So my cinema is expensive because I have to construct everything in the studio. Where else could I produce my fantasies? And this should not be misconstrued as a *capriccio* on my part.

PSYCHIC SCARS

It's clear that an artist draws his inspiration directly from his own traumatism, from the wounds and scars of his psychic experience. Various forms of neurosis have a providential function for the creative individual…. I would say that neurosis has a providential nature in that it constitutes a deposit, a storehouse, or an antechamber of treasures where an artist can draw upon all the stories ever imagined, as in those fairy-tales that describe a fabulous treasure buried at the bottom of the sea or hidden in a cavern guarded by monsters, by dragons, that the hero must first vanquish if he is to merit the wealth inside. In general, the creative person must drag out into the light one of these jewels, a portion of this treasure, the thing that's hidden. Naturally, he must expose himself to the dangers posed by the infernal guardians, the satanic ones. It is precisely this danger that the artist identifies as the neurotic, psychotic aspect of his artistic endeavor, as we find in the great tradition of accursed artists like Baudelaire, Van Gogh, Poe, all of whom paid a very high price for having come too close to certain truths without having the knowledge, the protection, of psychoanalysis. They didn't have what was necessary to make an asbestos suit that could protect them from this fiery, magnetic dimension. No, personally, I think I've been very lucky: apart from various indispensable and nourishing bouts with depression, I don't have any stigmata to show you!

PUPPETS

The relationship between a director and his actors is like that between the puppeteer and his puppets. It's collaboration: the puppets are happy to be puppets if the puppeteer is a good master. I have never had problems with actors, even with the most temperamental ones simply because I love actors—I've always loved them. I find them immensely sympathetic. I love their infantile caprices, their childishness, their peacock extroversion… Psychologically, they're fascinating. I can be very physical with my actors, but it's not just to get what I want from them: I try to create an atmosphere of confidence on the set and so I'm very affectionate with them. My earliest memory of an actor was at the theater, the moment when the actors—all unknowns—first appeared on stage. I'd seen their faces on posters announcing the play and when they appeared—they seemed like divinities, extraterrestrials. I had only to accept them and to love them.

RECIPE FOR A GOOD FILM

A good opening and a good ending make for a good film provided they come close together.

RHINOCEROS MILK

Mother's milk is a very Italian image that I've used once or twice in my films. Woman is an ambassador, a mediator, and thus a powerful stimulus. In *And the Ship Sails On*, rhinoceros's milk has connotations of something unconsciously buried in man that, if neglected, would fester and poison him. The subconscious is fed by confusion, by the unexpected, by the perpetually immobile—and that frightens us. But that's why we should explore these obscure zones. To ignore the subconscious is to mutilate oneself. ¶ The ending of *And the Ship Sails On* with Freddie Jones espousing the nourishing quality of rhinoceros milk is based on a personal habit of mine. I start every morning with a tall glass of rhinoceros milk specially flown in from Kenya and the beneficial effects are amazing—I'm sprouting a new crop of hair on my head.

RITUALS

A film director is probably more protected than other artists in contact with the unconscious. He's protected by a ritual that he practices unconsciously the moment he enters a film studio: the ritual of discussions with his troupe, the ritual involved in switching the projectors on and off, the ritual of screen tests and rehearsals, the ritual behind each phase of the film, the ritual of encouraging a continuous scenographic and choreographic invention, the ritual of pretending, of fabricating a fake sea, a fake field, a fake storm—all this unconscious energy devoted to the gods of fiction and representation is simply the repetition of a magic ritual of protection that allows what must appear to appear. A film director is Mandrake with a camera for a wand.

Gelsomina, the Chaplin-inspired character immortalized by Giulietta Masina. (*La Strada*, 1954)

Fellini on set setting up the hysterical kitchen scene. (*Amarcord*, 1973)

SCRIPTS

I was still searching for the lead role in *La Dolce Vita* when I asked Marcello to come to my summerhouse in Fregene, telling him I needed a nondescript face for my new film. He arrived on time and then very politely asked if he could read the script. Flaiano had come up earlier in the day and was installed outside on a hammock in the shade. I motioned for him to show Marcello the script. It was a tome of three hundred pages, a mass of blank loose-leaf paper containing the drawing of a man seated in a lotus position on the surface of the ocean with his sexual member hanging way down to the bottom of the sea. Swimming around it, like Esther Williams, were these beautiful buxom mermaids. "Yes, yes," said Marcello excitedly, "very interesting! I accept the role!"

SENSE OF TOUCH

The sense of touch is important to me. For example, drapery—the quality of its fabric—is something that concerns me personally because it's part of the overall painting. A painter can't designate someone else to hold his brush: the expression must be his own. And so this also applies to film, which is painting more than it is literature or theater. Filmmaking is all about objects and how light falls onto the objects you've arranged in space. ¶ *But how does this tactility operate?* ¶ By touching everything you come in contact with. In the arrangement of a wig, in applying makeup, devising a wax chin or gauging the difference in texture between one kind of silk and another. I feel that I must inhabit and exert control over the decor down to the last detail. If I had to narrate this room, for example, naturally I would have to choose the colors, manufac-

Il Maestro showing how he wants the ironing done at the Feminists' Convention. (*City of Women*, 1980)

ture the light fixtures, and construct the sofa. And then I would need to live in it, to *inhale* the room—including the adjoining rooms—even during breaks in production. I would need to impregnate myself in this room and for the room to impregnate itself in me before I could feel comfortable about inventing a story around it. ¶ *A continuous process. At home as well?* ¶ You mean, do I like moving the furniture around? No, because Giulietta won't let me! ¶ *Oh, but you'd love to, Federico.* ¶ No, no. ¶ *Yes, yes. Change everything: the beds, the furniture…* ¶ No, really. ¶ *The cushions…* ¶ No, no, I insist. At home, my manual capacities are completely immobilized. I wouldn't know how to hang a picture, heat coffee, turn on the TV, whereas in the studio, I'm cook, upholsterer, interior decorator, locksmith, prop man, best boy, anesthetist…. I become omniscient, ultrareliable, because I'm at the center of my own truth, my own reality. However, I don't want to give you the idea that a filmmaker is some kind of semidivine creature. I regret having to confess it this way. But it's true that, for a film, I have to create everything from scratch: characters, objects, decor, landscape. For example, *The Voice of the Moon* started off as a vague idea. I was inspired by Ermanno Cavazzoni's novel *Il Poema dei Lunatici*, but I took only a vibration, a suggestion, the ghost of a purpose from it. In order to make it my own, I felt it was necessary to build an entire country. So I mobilized the whole of Cinecittà to construct my story. I built a piazza, a church, a discothèque, a town hall, a shopping mall, markets, outfitting each boutique with its own floor tiles, and tiles for the roof. I saw the necessity of building a world that conformed to my vision of life using the various expressive means that I consider indispensable. Next, I had to inhabit this world, placing people in windows, a news vendor in the kiosk, a tobacconist in the café, a hairdresser in the salon. The film wasn't contained only in a sound, a voice, or a certain intensity of light.

Rome, June 18, 1941: Fellini's father, Urbano, with the director's younger sister, Maddalena.

No, I had to construct sound and lighting from scratch. Once completed, I could stand back and look at it, observe the characters and the decor, and then invent a story involving hundreds of people by watching them live, by obliging them to come and stand in their places. It's the very opposite of what you'd expect from a film director! I constructed an entire world for *The Voice of the Moon* and by studying it day after day with great curiosity—by being attentive to it in the manner of the journalist, the detective, or the vagabond—and by choosing the characters one by one, by costuming each one of them and giving them lines to read, I created the authentic life of a little country. And the film is precisely about that life.

SENSORY STIMULI

To establish the proper frame of mind to create, Schiller claimed he needed the odor of melons rotting near his work-table, while Turgenev liked to soak his feet in a bucket of hot water. Balzac's stimulus was drinking toxic quantities of coffee. This is a stupid question, but I was wondering if you had recourse to anything as outlandish? ¶ Yes, Balduin Babbuìno's Amazing Hair Tonic. My father, Urbano, recommended it, it was a product he sold. Every day before work, he swabbed his balding pate with Babbuìno's, daubing a few drops behind his ears and when Mom wasn't looking, laced his morning coffee with it. In this way, Dad left the house in a bright and peppy—what is the word?—heady, creative mood. ¶ Ask me a stupid question and you'll get a commercial! And so, although I respect the extravagant needs of these great artists I don't require a sensory stimulus to get me going…. Still, the sight of a beautiful woman standing on a street corner, perceived from the limousine taking me to Cinecittà … her smile…. A pleasant female incarnation is a wonderful incentive,

Fellini discussing a scene with Roberto Benigni, who plays the inspired simpleton Ivo Salvini. (*The Voice of the Moon*, 1990)

but it's not a necessity! Our conversations ripe with silly questions and brainless answers are equally stimulating and certainly more agreeable than rancid melon rinds, buckets of coffee, and soaking feet! On the other hand, a gorgeous brunette eating melon and sipping coffee, with her toes in a bucket of water, now that's what I'd call a *real* stimulus.

SERIOUS THINKING

I have the impression that I never do any thinking on my own—serious thinking, I mean. My best ideas come in conversations with sensitive interlocutors—and cynics like Daumier in *8 ½*—just as my best direction is done when I'm in the midst of a chaotic but marvelous troupe of actors and technicians.

SHAKESPEARE

Ennio Flaiano introduced me to Shakespeare. I would pick Flaiano up in my car and we'd drive to one of those rundown deserted bars that litter the beaches of Ostia. We'd order something to eat and drink and I would have him explain to me the subtlety of the great playwright's work, in particular, *King Lear*. One day during our talks, Flaiano stood up and, to the sound of the crashing waves, recited the unforgettable lines:

> Hark, did you hear the news? King Lear fell off a cliff.
> O horrible! Were you very close to him?
> Indeed, sir, close enough to push.

Shooting the canal scene with lighting genius Giuseppe Rotunno (kneeling) in which Casanova (Donald Sutherland) is seduced by a beautiful black man, a controversial sequence cut from the final version. (*Fellini's Casanova*, 1976)

But seriously, *Othello* inflamed my imagination. Iago and Othello are like twin brothers in a Brothers Grimm fairy tale where one denies the other with dire consequences. And, by chance, they happen to resemble clowns. Othello is the White Clown who incarnates elegance, harmony, intelligence, and nobility of soul. Iago is the Auguste, the evil Black Clown who rebels against the perfection of the White Clown. Bruno Bettelheim said that tragedy occurs when the two disparate aspects of our personality cannot be integrated. That is a very Jungian idea. And also, Blake's Contraries are at work in the play's dialectics of Black and White, Good and Evil. Othello and Iago are two sides, then, of the same coin, two tragic heroes. Together, they form "the beast with two backs," a very sexual metaphor. To my mind, the secret of the play is the blackness of the Moor, a secret similar to the whiteness of the whale in *Moby-Dick*. Now, up to a certain point, Othello is the noble Moor but by the play's end, Emilia describes him as "ignorant as dirt," that is, the color of dirt. When Iago says, "I would change my humanity for a baboon," in the Elizabethan spectator's mind, the baboon was a slur meant for Othello. But since Iago has no humanity, the baboon is Iago— poor baboon! Iago's blind imperative is to destroy Othello: "We are the same—you are no better than myself." Like the White Clown and the Auguste, the two are linked and feed off each other: in destroying Othello, Iago will destroy himself and vice versa. Herein lies the paradox of what I call the tragedy of tragedy in *Othello*: by marrying Desdemona, Othello attempts to unite the disparate aspects of his personality, but the Auguste in him, embodied by Iago, refuses this union and so tragedy cannot be avoided. ¶ There is a simple but telling question at the heart of the play: Why would an aging, world-weary black general in the Machiavellian city of Venice fall in love with a young, white Venetian lady who clearly has knowledge of the

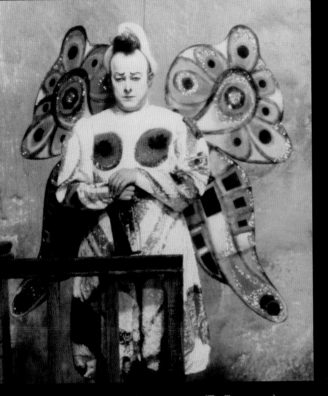

lowns and clowning: celebrating a dying institution. (*The Clowns*, 1970)

ourtesan's ways of the world? Why? In order to unite opposites that cannot be united and so bring about ragedy. Desdemona falls in love with his mind, he falls for her physical beauty, that is, her whiteness—not er innocence—for the question of her innocence is what plagues him at the back of his mind. Othello ecomes the Beauty's Black, Desdemona the Black's Beauty, but their marriage is never consummated. So ow we have a play about Beauty and the Beast, the Beast who will finally reveal himself to Beauty as he truly s, that is, Iago the Black Beast—for no Iago, however demoniacally Machiavellian, however dark a threat odged in Othello's unconscious, can alone drive a truly pure spirit to murder if he already did not possess uch desires. This is where black Othello is white Iago, confirming the white in black and the black in white: he "beast with two backs." ¶ For a film inspired by the play, I would need to create a typical circus situation n which the clowns' makeup and costumes would require the following: Iago—an Auguste in white face and olorful rags, left leg chained to a tiny black heart that he drags in the dust with ease. Othello— White Clown n black face and regal white costume, right leg chained to a giant white heart immobilizing him. ¶ By film's nd, Othello is blown out of a cannon as the terrifying Green-Eyed Monster and into the dying arms of esdemona. What does this monster look like? Why, an Auguste, of course. ¶ The next great author Flaiano nd I discussed was John Milton. I learned that the blind poet wrote *Paradise Lost* and *Paradise Regained*, the atter written after his wife died. This came as no surprise. Hadn't Socrates poisoned himself with wedlock?

SNAKES AND LADDERS

t was in Turin, the city of his employer Einaudi, that Calvino first saw *8 ½* at the 1963 premiere and

Edmea Tetua (Janet Suzman) as the mysterious opera diva in a scene cut from the final version. (*And the Ship Sails On*, 1983)

soon afterward sent me a short, affectionate letter expressing his admiration. I was flattered, profoundly moved that such a brilliant writer would find my work worthy of his interest. I called him and we arranged to meet at Canova's in Piazza del Popolo. Together, over coffee, we hatched a film project that dealt with fables as prophetic dreams inspired by his classic text, *Italian Folktales*. You have to remember that this was during a time when movies, projected onto huge screens in a darkened amphitheater, still held an awesome power to hypnotize the spectator and transport him to another world, unlike television that drastically reduces his field of vision to a luminous spot in a corner of the room. The film would narrate the fabulous, visionary aspects of an Italy perceived as the pleasure dome of Kubla Khan. But then Calvino moved to Paris and although we telephoned each other, we lost the habit of working on the screenplay. Our work method was a relaxed one: it consisted of rarely meeting up to compare and discuss our notes but instead writing whenever we felt inspired, in the knowledge that sooner or later an overpowering idea would take hold and the subsequent enthusiasm force us to arrange a meeting either at my office in the Corso d'Italia or else at Canova's. It was only when he returned to settle in Rome for good that we resumed our collaboration on the tentatively titled *Visions Italy*. In the long interim of his self-imposed exile, I'd invented a snakes-and-ladders motif based on technology my special effects crew developed for *And the Ship Sails On* that united, in a fantastic and dreamlike way, the seven individual stories comprising the whole of our film. For example, the castle the fable called *The King Who Lived Next Door to a King* moves forward on gigantic camera tracks out of its mythological landscape to slide into the Gulf of Naples, its palace terrace awash in the Tyrrhenian Se-

Criticizing contemporary society: Ivo Salvini (Roberto Benigni) in a vision of lost harmony and genuine human communication. (*The Voice of the Moon*, 1990)

Here, under the shadow of Vesuvius, begins the tale called *The Queen of the Amputated Rib*. Sadly, tragically, it was during the production of *Ginger and Fred*, in 1985, that I learned of his death—a great loss for Italian culture. Both of us had agreed that Italian cinema was rapidly declining, that our culture had become a commodity.

SOLITUDE

The modern dilemma is solitude. No public celebration or political symphony can hope to be rid of it. Only through individuals can this solitude be broken, can a message be passed, making them understand the profound link that binds one person to another. It's what I tried to express in my last film, *The Voice of the Moon*, and it's what I tried to say in *La Strada* so many years ago. The feelings haven't changed. In *La Strada*, I tried to show the personal and supernatural communication between a man and a woman who would seem by nature to be the least likely people to understand each other.

SPONTANEITY

Creating is something we do unconsciously. An excessive awareness of the processes through which a creator realizes his work isn't helpful in the end and can, in fact, impede, interrupt that flow of fundamental energy, vital and indispensable, that we call for lack of anything better, spontaneity....
Spontaneity is the secret of life.

Archetypal clown images: Giulietta Masina as Gelsomina. (*La Strada*, 1954)

STAGNATION

Since *And the Ship Sails On*—which was a disaster—there's been a three-or four-year hiatus between each of my films. During that period, I'm very unhappy. I envy painters because they can paint their whole lives long. They go into the atelier, heat up a little tomato soup and then live and work more or less tranquilly, like a tree during the four seasons. They have a constant and genuine identification with their artistic means of expression. So to get through these periods of stagnation, I'd like to do everything: take photographs, shoot commercials, direct short films, conceive Punchinello theatricals in public parks, bang a drum, tap dance, sing.

THE STRANGE AND BEAUTIFUL

One autumn, while playing in the courtyard of an abandoned villa in Rimini, the frozen lunar features of a mentally handicapped child suddenly appeared in an upper-story window. I stopped playing at once and stared at him; he stared back a moment and was suddenly pulled away from the window. Trembling with fear, I ran all the way home: I was frightened yet fascinated by the apparition. The next day, a windy morning, I had my brother Riccardo accompany me to the courtyard. Among the wildly swaying trees, we discovered the anonymous child in the courtyard chaperoned by two very old, tender, and affectionate women dressed in black. Despite his drooling mouth, the outsized head, the empty eyes, I was no longer afraid of him. Clapping his hands and laughing, he chased—as best he could—the crisp dry leaves swirling at his feet. Riccardo and I were witnesses to an "extra-ordinary" reality—one that went against our normal bourgeois upbringing: in

Swinging sixties: Ascilto (Hiram Keller) in a favorite Fellini metaphor of unbridled sensuality. (*Fellini's Satyricon*, 1969)

this enchanted courtyard out of time, we had stumbled onto a truth of nature. Years later, while writing the script of *La Strada*, I remembered my strange and beautiful child and named him Osvaldo.

STREET SINGERS

I have always maintained that the critics have placed me too high on their list of directors. If I had the force to express myself with greater conviction, I'd be the head of a political party, a prophet, a saint, or the devil incarnate. I'm a *cantastorie*, a lowly street singer.

STYLE

I don't think style is a rational choice. The first rush of creativity contains the form the film will eventually assume, just as it does in a dream. Sometimes I can't remember all of a dream but the light, the atmosphere, the colors, the feeling that lingers afterward, are enough to tell me what the dream meant—the message seems contained in these primary elements the moment I wake up. So the style has already been determined and it's up to me to translate it into a film by using the tricks of my trade and an extreme sense of rigor. Otherwise it's lost in the course of filming. ¶ *Is it necessary that a film director invent his own style?* ¶ I don't know if someone could feel obliged to be original. Originality is something you have or you don't. You can't go and buy it somewhere.

Fellini explaining how to reprimand a delinquent student under Mussolini's Fascist gaze. (*Fellini's Roma*, 1972)

Ghosts from the past: Juliet's childhood memory of her role as a Roman martyr in a school play is used to explain her adult role as a submissive housewife. (*Juliet of the Spirits*, 1965)

TALISMAN

In *Juliet of the Spirits*, there's a scene where a troubled and confused Giulietta suddenly leaves Suzy's house after being wooed by an androgynous young man and bolts down a flight of stairs. If you look closely, there's a long winding crack in the wall. Inside the crack are the words, *asa nisi masa masina mastorna mastroianni*, which I'd painted in gold as a talisman.

TARZAN

It was a project conceived and written by Marcello Mastroianni sometime in 1986, I think, and one he suggested I direct: *Tarzan in Siberia*. Marcello's Tarzan is an Italian soldier who's remained behind in Siberia after the Second World War—he's unaware that it's ended. Physically, he's falling apart, with ulcers eating away his legs, advanced arthritis due to the extreme cold, and impotence, naturally the worst affliction of all. But he manages to survive on rations, black bread, and snow water that he melts in his fist, scrounging with the astute cleverness of mythical survivors like Crusoe and Gulliver, the Swiss Family Robinson, eventually adopting a baby polar bear he names Cheetah. Unwittingly, Tarzan stumbles into a concentration camp. In this arctic Sahara of lost souls, he meets Andrei Sakharov who revels in Tarzan's absurd sense of humor and the antics of Cheetah. Sakharov confesses his secret wish: to escape to Alaska and to freedom. Together, they hatch a plot but Sakharov dies before they can execute the plan. Tarzan decides his salvation is to head east for the Bering Strait. That evening, Russian soldiers place Sakharov's body in a coffin, expecting to bury him the following morning, but Tarzan manages to remove his friend's

The Devil disguised as a beautiful girl. (*Toby Dammit*, 1968)

body. He and Cheetah scramble inside the coffin, are carried outside and buried in shallow ground, then dig themselves out again. With only a frozen tin of corned beef, a rifle, and three bullets, they set out as night falls, but the dark is lit by a full moon. In the distance, Tarzan can make out the dense cloud of steam from a train heading east. Grabbing Cheetah in his arms, firing all three bullets into the air, he runs head-long toward the train, howling. And as the train approaches, he can make out in the icy yellow light of a window, Jane, the Russian heroine, a kind of Anna Karenina except that this is a felliniesque peasant girl with ankles and arms like a colossus, the kind that paves roads in a blizzard. Jane sees the half-frozen ape-man and it's love at first sight. "Come here, my darling baby! Come!" she yells, and revives him with her thick and nourishing peasant's milk.… It's supposed to be a fable about old age and solitude. ¶ *Did you refuse to direct the film because you hadn't collaborated on the script?* ¶ No, I just didn't look forward to shooting those winter scenes with a polar bear! And besides, Marco Ferreri would have done a much better job.

TELEVISION

In The Voice of the Moon, *you're particularly ferocious with the younger generation. At seventy-two, would you say that you have a tendency to disagree with what the young do?* ¶ The young watch television twenty-four hours a day, they don't read and they rarely listen. This incessant bombardment of images has developed a hypertrophied eye condition that's turning them into a race of mutants. They should pass a law for a total reeducation of the young, making children visit the Galleria Borgese on a daily basis. ¶ *Susan Sontag believes television is worse than heroin.* ¶ Generally speaking, I think television has betrayed the meaning of

Toby Dammit (Terence Stamp) offering his head in exchange for a Ferrari. (*Toby Dammit*, 1968)

democratic speech, adding visual chaos to the confusion of voices. What role does silence have in all this noise? *La Dolce Vita* announced the arrival of the consumer society in Italy. *Ginger and Fred* was an attempt to narrate the mutation of our society into one where the myths we need to survive and once had in popular culture have degenerated into game shows where someone with more teeth than a piano spins a wheel shouting, "My kingdom for a microwave oven!" By replacing experience with this unending flow of obdurate electronic images, we've grown dependent on a virtual reality that is simply a fancy term for an eye laxative. Cinema has the capacity to offer us a high density of meaning by mobilizing each gesture, each color, each word, each element into a single powerful image. Television, on the contrary, can offer only the meaning of the facts that are being transmitted.

TERENCE STAMP

Antonioni had fired Terencino from *Blow Up* and the actor was hanging on in Roma, hoping for his next big break. Bernardino Zapponi and I had just finished the script to *Toby Dammit* and, by chance, someone handed me a photograph of Stamp with that extraordinarily angelic yet abysmally decadent face of his: the perfect loser-dandy, the Dionysian rock star, the alcoholic aristocrat rotting from within yet capable of working his blond, monumental charm. You know, someone I could identify with, my alter ego. We arranged a meeting and I hired him on the spot. One day, during shooting, I was getting my hair cut when Antonioni walked in and sat down in the barber's chair beside me. "I hear you're working with Stamp," he said. "My sympathies." "*Grazie mille*, Michelangelo," I replied. "Thanks to you, I discovered a genius."

Creating the illusion of vast winter landscapes that mirror Casanova's fear of old age, solitude, and impotence. (*Fellini's Casanova*, 1976)

THUNDER AND LIGHTNING

Disasters excite me. When I was a child, an approaching storm, the thunder and lightning, the torrents of rain, the trembling walls, would send me into fits of ecstasy. So I'm not discouraged by the contemporary atmosphere of total decadence, of worlds collapsing, of a *dolce vita* not so *dolce*. On the contrary, it forces me to be attentive, to witness the apocalypse, to narrate it in a film after experiencing it. I would like just one thing: to be permitted to live a little longer to tell the tale.

TIME PASSING

I don't have the sensation of time passing. I can't give you dates. I can only cite films as reference points for such-and-such a period of my life, so much so that when someone asks me a question in which I have to supply a precise year, to remember, I think of the film I was making at that time. It's as though I have always made films. This point of reference is an eternal present. Time has stopped, immobilized, and I have the impression that it's always the same day, that I've always been inside a movie studio, megaphone in hand, shouting, cajoling, playing the clown, the police commissioner, the general, the charlatan. And suddenly the memories of the past forty years reappear in front of me, surrounded in darkness and light— the darkness above, the light below—like a succession of moving shadows that I must arrange in space.... It seems that my life has burned and will go on burning in this image of obscurity and light. And so, I don't have the sensation of time passing, even less of time, slowly but surely, running out.

Sandra Milo as Fanny, the circus performer.
(*Juliet of the Spirits*, 1965)

Aggressive prostitutes hustling for trade in a working-class brothel. (*Fellini's Roma*, 1972)

TOULOUSE-LAUTREC

Henri de Toulouse-Lautrec is a painter dear to my heart. Circuses, fairs, puppets, music hall, prostitutes, bordellos—all the things I like—fascinated him. He would have made a master cameraman: his compositions were guided by intuition and emotion first, while aesthetic concerns came second. He knew nothing about good taste and would have loathed the invention of ketchup and kitsch. He possessed the infallible intuition of the born filmmaker. He was an immensely gifted freak—a great big head on a tiny body—who transformed an infirmity into gold, as any neurotic with an inferiority complex must, and I'm no exception. When I restructured Donaldino's face for *Casanova*, I felt Toulouse-Lautrec was guiding my hand, as though we were remodeling *Valentin le Désossé*.

TRANSPLANTS

I thought of making a film about a very wealthy but very nasty middle-aged aristocrat whose corrupt ways have rotted his heart. He undergoes a heart transplant, receiving the vital young heart of a kind and beautiful woman, like one of those Hammer horror films where the mad surgeon invents a technique for grafting hands and ends up having a murderer's hand grafted onto his own amputated one. Of course, a hand is important, but a heart is the organ of our emotions, the center of the soul—the *animatus* if you want to get Latin about it. Plato insisted that the soul was an eternal substance and I tend to side with him and not Aristotle, who claimed it was the invisible form of a living body that disappeared when the body died. Both of these ideas are pretty wild, but Plato seems the more fantastic and so naturally the one I prefer. ¶ Anyway, this thin, choleric, nasty little man is taken

Casanova (Donald Sutherland) as the champion of sexual athleticism and masculine stupidity. (*Fellini's Casanova*, 1976)

home from the hospital in an ambulance. Slowly, he recovers his strength. His appetite improves and he puts on some weight, first in his wasted arms and legs. Soon, however, his butt gets rounder and he starts developing pectorals that, over the next few weeks, and to his great dismay, develop into humongous, voluptuous breasts. His male member shrinks overnight into a bona fide vagina. His doctors can't figure out what the problem is and want to inject him full of testosterone, but the nasty man refuses. He's beginning to like his new body. And the few friends he has are witness to a miraculous change in him: no more the Fascist Italian Scrooge but a sort of gorgeous Mother Teresa eager to share his millions, for even his face has taken on the sexy Madonna features of a Sophia Loren. The villagers, disconcerted and suspicious at first, are now perfectly willing to overlook the transformation of man into woman, especially if the woman is beautiful and generous. The village peasants are given access to his, or rather, her, vast estates, where they cultivate corn, wheat, and vineyards. In exchange, they shower her with cornucopias. ¶ One day, she goes for a walk in the fields and sees a young man harvesting the corn. They exchange glances as though they'd met before, perhaps in another lifetime. She invites him to her castle. Over dinner, they discover they are indeed kindred souls. She falls in love—for the first time in her sad, pathetic life—with the handsome, robust peasant: a young, athletic man with strong arms and a pale, romantic face like Robert Taylor or Tyrone Power. That night, they make love and the very next day, the young man moves into the castle for a month of perfect happiness. That's when the news hits her: the valves of her vital young heart are now mysteriously clogged with fatty tissues. Tests are performed but the doctors are baffled once again. What could be killing her? It would seem, the villagers whisper, that she's killing herself with kindness. And so the film ends on a tragic note when a dark, mysterious woman with a pale, romantic face arrives in the village

announcing that the young man is the son she bore after being ravished by the woman who was once a man. ¶ How we interpret this story isn't what intrigues me. What holds my interest is the nature of the metamorphosis and how to achieve that transformation in film—the creation of a fantastic atmosphere where the lighting, the shadows, the silences reveal the profound meaning behind the tale. Kafka's *Metamorphosis* is fascinating, but you'd make a big mistake if, for the screen, you focused on its message.

TWO FILMS IN ONE

I always direct two films simultaneously. During several weeks, the first film—the one I'm supposed to be making—remains a mystery to me despite the elaborate scenario. The second film, however, serves as preparation for the first, a sort of fake film I use to fool the producers but one that is absolutely essential to the first. It's an artistic process, of course, that makes editing my films a rather complicated affair. Grace to their expertise, my editor Nino Baragli and two professional, highly maternal assistants contribute to making the atmosphere in the cutting room a festive and joyous one, but I alone decide image after image, meter after meter, sequence after sequence, since the editing itself was completed each day in my mind while filming my two films.

TWO LIVES

We live two lives—one with our eyes open and one with them closed. Eyes open are for perceiving the exterior universe. Eyes shut are for exploring the inner cosmos. I spend all day with my eyes shut bumping into people and things. That's why I don't drive anymore.

Inveterate skirt chaser Fausto (Franco Fabrizi, left) with friends Alberto (Alberto Sordi, backseat), Leopoldo (Leopoldo Trieste, in glasses), and Riccardo (Riccardo Fellini) searching for Sandra, Fausto's estranged wife. (*I Vitelloni*, 1953)

Fellini with Michelangelo Antonioni at Cinecittà during the ill-fated production. (*Fellini's Casanova*, 1976)

VAGABONDS AND THE CIRCUS

There is only one place where the phenomenal, excess, and the extreme exist without vulgarity: in the equestrian circus. For me, it remains the summit of popular entertainment. In this fabulous world of color, movement, and emotion we rediscover the eternal vagabond for whom Chaplin loaned his face. Half angel, half demon, the vagabond possesses the philosopher's wisdom, the cat's vitality, the sleep-walker's awkward grace. If he projects light, he also conserves an impenetrable shadow—the true source of his constant fascination. The vagabond reminds me of my childhood, of Pinocchio, of Bibo and Arcibaldo, two famous comic strip characters published in the *Corriere dei piccoli*. As a child, I'd place the newspaper on the glass of my bedroom window and spend hours tracing Bibo and Arcibaldo until the sun went down.... I would say that Cabiria, certainly Gelsomina and even Ivo Salvini are based on early memories of Pinocchio and the circus and possibly Dickensian inventions like David Copperfield and Oliver Twist, whom I adored.

VISCONTI AND ANTONIONI

I don't see any possibility of establishing a parallel between my films and those of Visconti. He's a great filmmaker, a superb narrator, but he made films in a more illustrative manner than I do. He was a long-distance illustrator, powerful, like a nineteenth-century novelist. In this sense, he was a master. ¶ Antonioni is like a scientist in his approach to filmmaking, taking the world as his laboratory and examining it under a microscope. His acute powers of observation interpret a reality where cause and effect are

Sacred and profane: Fellini's giant Madonna-Whore balloon of male sexual fantasy. (*City of Women*, 1980)

shrouded in mystery, in the profound ambiguity that characterizes the work of all great artists. The more we think we know, *the less we know.* And I think a lot of young filmmakers should take him as a magnificent example of humility.

VOICES AND FACES

There is an image in Dante that has haunted me ever since I first read him as a young man during the war and which haunts me now that I'm old. It's in the passage where Brunetto Latini's ghostly voice is heard crying out of the dark wall of smoke concealing him, a bit like God's voice out of the Burning Bush. Dante recognizes the voice, he identifies it merely by its timbre. In the same way, I would argue that there are forgotten faces, even unknown faces that you recognize by the quality of their timbre. It would be worth the challenge to try and achieve in film what Dante so effortlessly obtained with the voice of Brunetto Latini: making the invisible visible.

VOYAGE TO TULUM

It ended up a wild goose chase, searching for Carlos Castaneda. I flew to Los Angeles in the hope of seeing him after fibbing to journalists that I'd first met him in Rome in 1977. Anyway, I'd finished *City of Women* and wanted desperately to follow up with my pet project based on the work of the famous anthropologist. ¶ I must have contacted everyone connected to him but all they could tell me was that it was impossible to meet him. One day, a man called me at my hotel saying he was Carlos Castaneda. ¶ "Is that so?" I said wearily. ¶

A camera crew masked like speleologists discovering a lost chamber of ancient Roman frescoes beneath the city's subway line. (*Fellini's Roma*, 1972)

"At lunch today, you were served by a tall, elegant waiter, a thin, bald man with black eyes and a dark moustache." ¶ "My friend," I said even more wearily, "that could be just about any waiter in the world." ¶ He said, "Yes, but in your mind you heard a voice whisper, 'You have come to meet the Mescaline Man.' " ¶ I almost dropped the receiver. ¶ "Who are you?" I said, my voice trembling. ¶ "C.C.," he said, "at your service. Perhaps we will meet again but certainly not before you have been initiated. For this to happen, you must first travel to Mexico." ¶ Mescaline Man hung up. ¶ The next day, I flew to Mexico City. Sure enough, in the days that followed, I experienced a suite of events that, to put it mildly, were out of this world. I started getting bizarre telephone calls made by the strangest voices communicating in the oddest accented English. I would ask, "But who are you?" and the voices answered, "We are beings who have never been incarnated in men." At worst, I took them for a gang of practical jokers, at best a society of expert magicians having fun at my expense. Imagine my surprise when the voices revealed secrets to me that I have never revealed to anyone. It was uncanny, uncomfortable, profoundly disturbing. ¶ They then began communicating in the oddest Italian, explaining that their efforts were to "translate into human words news of an inhuman world." ¶ "*Bravissimo!*" I told them. "But all I want just now is to meet Carlos Castaneda. Do you think that's possible?" ¶ "No," they said. "You cannot meet what you do not understand." ¶ "When will I understand?" ¶ "The next time you meet C.C.," they said and hung up. ¶ Three days later, I met my waiter again—Carlos Castaneda—who immediately agreed to take me on a voyage of initiation to the land of the Toltec sorcerers. At last, I rejoiced, a dream come true! Now I can make my film about a film director who, with Castaneda as his guide, sets out on the initiatory voyage that the anthropologist himself had undertak-

An entire Roman piazza complete with tramway tracks constructed at Cinecittà's enormous Teatro 5. (*Fellini's Roma*, 1972)

en. Here was a project dear to my heart: for the first time in forty years, I would film outside Cinecittà, and for the first time in my life, beyond Europe. It was going to be a real challenge to see whether I could make a film far from the protective forces of Cinecittà's Studio 5, of Roma, of Italy, of my home with Giulietta. Carlos and I arranged to meet the following day: there was a good deal of work ahead of us. ¶ And that's when he disappeared, this time for good, at which point, things got very complicated—how you say? The plot thickens. ¶ I was beginning to understand. ¶ Tullio [Pinelli] and I wrote up the story of my travels and searches in the wilds of Mexico, calling it *The Voyage to Tulum*, but we shelved it to make *Ginger and Fred*, a film destined to protect me from Berlusconi and his toxic television programs. *Tulum* was first published in 1986 in the *Corriere della serra* with drawings by Milo Manara. In this way, I could finally liquidate my fantasy of filming the "Amazing Adventures of Mescaline Man."

WHORES

Mamma puttana is the indispensable salutary counterpoint to every Italian *mamma mia*.

THE WOMAN-TREE

I once drew a caricature of myself happily asleep at the foot of a tall, pulpy tree with full, ripe breasts. This "Woman-Tree" provided shelter from the storm, from anxiety and guilt. It's a tree that curiously enough has its modest origins in the monstrous and genial "Man-Tree" of Hieronymous Bosch, a copy of which I'd first seen as a child in the art books of my Gambettola painter friends. Although it's a hellish vision, the image nonetheless evoked my longing for a tree house built with my Dad's help in the tallest tree on the front lawn. The blasted trunk of the "Man-Tree" contains a round table at which male and female figures have gathered to drink and celebrate. Bosch's image is no doubt the source of Susy's tree house hideaway in *Juliet of the Spirits*, except that I didn't have the budget to construct a giant head that swiveled back to observe with bemused detachment the sensual antics of Susy and her entourage. In fact, Bosch's creation is a splendid cinematic metaphor: it embodies my idea of the director carrying actors and decor inside his own body but who is himself contained within the body of his film.

WOMEN

For the Greeks, the grand construction of mythology gave us feminine figures bestowing divine benediction on favorites and shirts of flame for those they hated. They split the psychological makeup of woman into a host of composites that include Minerva, the intellectual goddess, and Diana, the huntress and warrior—incarnating

Fellini's first color film initiated a
new departure: a deeply introspective
cinematic style influenced by dreams.
(*The Temptations of Dr. Antonio*, 1962)

ABOVE AND OPPOSITE: In the pine forest near Fregene: Fellini demonstrating how he wants Marcello Mastrioanni (Snàporaz) to purse his lips for a kiss. Fellini then directing British actress Bernice Stegers (Mystery Woman) how to kiss an intimidated Snàporaz. The puppeteer demonstrating a more intimate and aggressive approach…and his puppets going through the motions. (*City of Women*, 1980)

woman's aggressive, competitive nature—or Venus, goddess of love and art. But there's a fact we often overlook: the Greek poet, before he sat down to write, addressed a prayer to his muse that she nourish him with inspiration, that she give him strength in the struggle with his imagination. In this way, women have always been the source of man's creativity. Woman is the representation of the eternal principle of creation, the yin in yang, the dark in light…. I'll find another cliché tomorrow, but for today, will this do? ¶ *Would you say you understand women?* ¶ No, but then do we ever really understand another person, leaving aside this problem of the sexes? ¶ *Do you fear women, Federico?* ¶ The word *fear* is somewhat exaggerated…. Curious, fascinated, enchanted by women, by a feeling of waiting, even if fear is an emotion that should be cultivated by a creative person. I think a man can't help being afraid because it's precisely this attitude of anxiety and waiting for something we don't know, perhaps will never know, that gives him a deeper meaning to life. Fear can be good, depending on how you deal with it. A man without fear is an idiot, a robot. It's an emotion intrinsic to humanity. If you consider fear in relation to women, I would say that it's the attitude that women suggest to men—not just to artists but also to men in general—more than this question of fear, that causes the confusion. Men project themselves onto women and women onto men, so there will always exist a deep misunderstanding between the sexes. I think we project onto women a feeling of waiting, something akin to a revelation, the arrival of a message, a little like the character in Kafka who waited in vain for the Emperor's word. A woman is like the Empress who has sent—who knows how many millions of years ago—a message that hasn't reached us yet. But this is a happy event because the taste for life is in waiting for the message and not in the message itself.

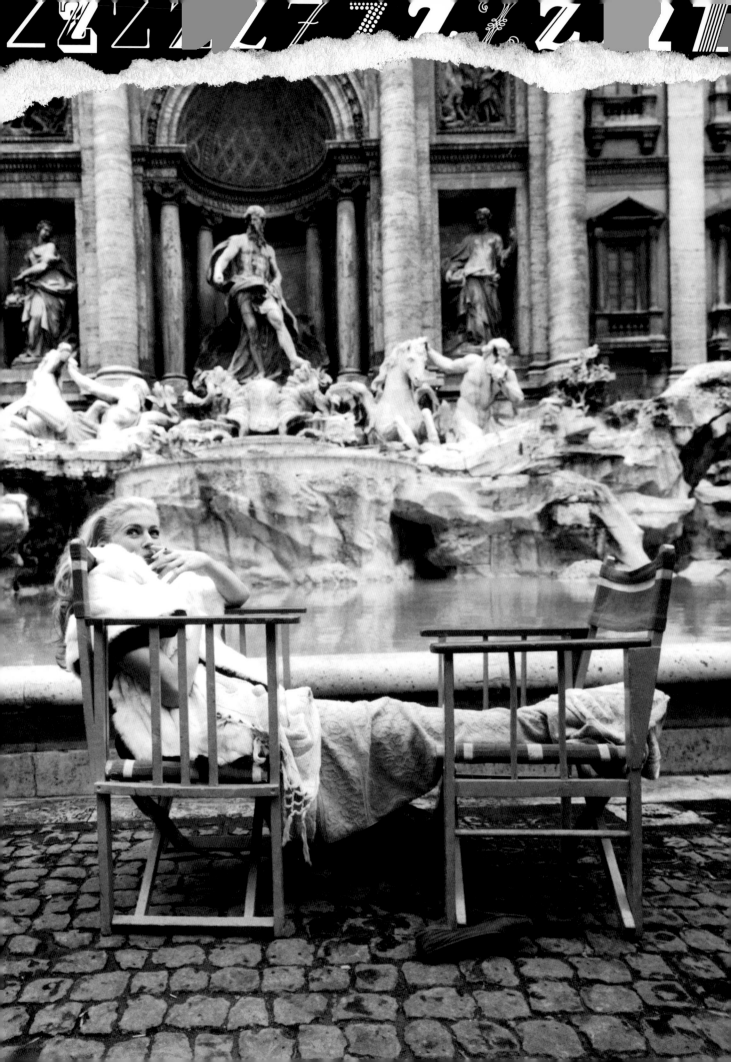

ZIO LUPO

The wolf is a powerful symbol in Italy, often seen as a beneficial intermediary between man and nature. For example, the wolf nourished Romulus and Remus. I myself was kidnapped by a wolf as a baby and brought up for a time in the jungles of Rimini. In Canto I of Dante's *Inferno*, the wolf is the initiating animal, appearing in a triad of animals: panther, lion, etc. Given that this lower triad corresponds to the upper Trinity, Dante has it reappear in Canto XXXIV as Satan with three heads. So the wolf also represents negative aggression, evil, and death. ¶ In a fairy tale from my native region of Romagna, the wolf gobbles up the greedy little girl. It is carnival time and everyone is eating pancakes except the little girl, who fell asleep. So she runs home crying to her mother. "Don't cry," says her mother, "I'll make you pancakes." But the family is so poor they don't have a frying pan. "*E!*" says her mother brightly. "Zio Lupo has a pan. Go and ask him to let us use it for a day." ¶ The little girl runs to Zio Lupo's house in the forest and asks to borrow the pan. ¶ "You can use my pan for a day but only if you promise to have Mamma return it filled with pancakes and brown ale." ¶ "I promise," says the little girl. ¶ Back home, her mother cooks piles of pancakes, enough for the whole family and Zio Lupo, too. "Remember the promise you made," says her mother. "Before night falls, you must return the pan filled with pancakes and a jug of brown ale." ¶ Halfway in the forest, the little girl can't resist the smell of the pancakes. "What harm can it do if I eat just one?" So she ate a pancake, washed it down with brown ale and continued on her way. But the taste was so good she decided to have another. "What harm can it do if I eat just one more?" So she had a second and third, a fourth and fifth, all washed down with brown ale until finally nothing was left in the pan but some crumbs. ¶ On the grass by the road lay some rabbit turds the size of her crumbs. With the flat of the pan, she pounded the turds and crumbs into new pancakes. In a puddle, she refilled the jug with muddy water. ¶ Zio Lupo received her graciously and sat down to his feast. First, he took a swig from the jug. "*Porca miseria!* This is muddy water!" Then he chomped into the pancake. "*Merda!* This is rabbit turd!" ¶ The greedy little girl took to her heels and flew out the door. "When the clock strikes midnight, I'm ready to bite!" cried Zio Lupo, shaking his fist after her. ¶ The greedy little girl ran all the way home and cried to her mother: "Mamma, Mamma! Come midnight, Zio Lupo's going to eat me!" So she and her mother rushed around the house, barricading the windows and doors. In the hearth, they lit a big fire should he try to slide down the chimney. And with that, the greedy little girl went to bed. ¶ But Zio Lupo came up the cellar stairs and just as the clock struck twelve, gobbled up the greedy girl—and her mother, too.

Films Directed by Fellini

1950

Luci del varietà (Variety Lights)
CODIRECTOR: Alberto Lattuada
STORY: Federico Fellini
SCRIPT: Alberto Lattuada, Federico Fellini, Tullio Pinelli, Ennio Flaiano
DIRECTOR OF PHOTOGRAPHY: Otello Martelli
SET DESIGN: Aldo Buzzi
MUSIC: Felice Lattuada
EDITING: Mario Bonotti
ASSISTANT DIRECTOR: Angelo D'Alessandro
EXECUTIVE PRODUCER: Mario Ingrami
PRODUCERS: Alberto Lattuada and Federico Fellini
DIRECTOR OF PRODUCTION: Bianca Lattuada
PRODUCTION: Capitolium Film (cooperative production)
PREMIERE: Italy, 1950
FORMAT: 35mm, black & white
APPROXIMATE RUNNING TIME: 100'

LEAD ACTORS:
Checco Dalmonte › Peppino De Filippo
Liliana Antonelli › Carla Del Poggio
Melina Amour › Giulietta Masina
Johnny › Johnny Kitzmiller
Conti (Liliana's lover) › Folco Lulli
The Comedian › Dante Maggio
The Fakir › Giulio Cali
Enzo La Rosa › Carlo Romano

1952

Lo sceicco bianco (The White Sheik)
STORY: Federico Fellini and Tullio Pinelli, from an idea by Michelangelo Antonioni
SCRIPT: Federico Fellini, Tullio Pinelli, Ennio Flaiano
DIRECTOR OF PHOTOGRAPHY: Arturo Gallea
CAMERAMAN: Antonio Belviso
SET DESIGN: Federico Fellini and Raffaello Tolfo
MUSIC: Nino Rota
SOUND: Armando Grilli and Walfredo Traversari
EDITING: Rolando Benedetti
ASSISTANT DIRECTOR: Stefano Ubezio
PRODUCER: Luigi Rovere
DIRECTOR OF PRODUCTION: Enzo Provenzale
PRODUCTION SECRETARY: Renato Panetuzzi
PRODUCTION: PDC-OFI
PREMIERE: Venice International Film Festival, 6 September 1952
FORMAT: 35mm, black & white
APPROXIMATE RUNNING TIME: 85'

LEAD ACTORS:
Wanda Cavalli (wife) › Brunella Bovo
Leopoldo Trieste (husband) › Ivan Cavalli
Fernando Rivoli (White Sheik) › Alberto Sordi
Cabiria (prostitute) › Giulietta Masina
Marilena Velardi › Fanny Marchiò
Fotoromanzo director › Ernesto Almirante
Ivan's uncle › Ettore Margadonna

1953

I vitelloni (I Vitelloni, The Young and the Passionate)
STORY: Federico Fellini, Ennio Flaiano, Tullio Pinelli, from a Fellini-Pinelli idea
SCRIPT: Federico Fellini, Tullio Pinelli, Ennio Flaiano
DIRECTOR OF PHOTOGRAPHY: Otello Martelli, Luciano Trasatti, Carlo Carlini
CAMERAMEN: Roberto Girardi and Franco Villa
SET DESIGN: Mario Chiari
COSTUMES: Margherita Marinari Bomarzi
MUSIC: Nino Rota
EDITING: Rolando Benedetti
ASSISTANT DIRECTOR: Moraldo Rossi
PRODUCER: Lorenzo Pegoraro
DIRECTOR OF PRODUCTION: Luigi Giacosi
PRODUCTION SECRETARY: Ugo Benvenuti
PRODUCTION: Peg Films (Rome) / Cité Films (Paris)
PREMIERE: Venice International Film Festival, 26 October 1953
FORMAT: 35mm, black & white
APPROXIMATE RUNNING TIME: 103'

LEAD ACTORS:
Moraldo › Franco Interlenghi
Fausto › Franco Fabrizi
Alberto › Alberto Sordi
Leopoldo › Leopoldo Trieste
Riccardo › Riccardo Fellini
Sandra › Eleonara Ruffo
Sandra's father › Enrico Viarisio
Fausto's father › Jean Brochard
Alberto's sister › Claude Farrell
Signor Michele › Carlo Romano
Giulia › Lida Baarova
Mystery Woman › Arlette Sauvage
Natali (the actor) › Achille Majeroni

Un'agenzia matrimoniale (A Marriage Agency), fourth episode in *Amore in città (Love in the City)*
STORY: Federico Fellini
SCRIPT: Federico Fellini, Tullio Pinelli
PHOTOGRAPHY: Gianni Di Venanzo
SET DESIGN: Gianni Polidori
MUSIC: Mario Nascimbene
EDITING: Eraldo Da Roma
ASSISTANT DIRECTOR: Luigi Vanzi
PRODUCER: Cesare Zavattini
PRODUCTION: Faro Film
PREMIERE: November 1953
FORMAT: 35mm, black & white
APPROXIMATE RUNNING TIME: 23'

LEAD ACTORS:
Reporter › Antonio Cifariello
Rossana › Livia Venturini

1954

La strada (La Strada)
STORY: Tullio Pinelli and Federico Fellini
SCRIPT: Tullio Pinelli and Federico Fellini, with collaboration of Ennio Flaiano
ARTISTIC ADVISOR: Brunello Rondi
DIRECTOR OF PHOTOGRAPHY: Otello Martelli

CAMERAMAN: Roberto Girardi
SET DESIGN: Mario Ravasco
COSTUMES: Margherita Marinari Bomarzi
SOUND: A. Calpini
MUSIC: Nino Rota
EDITING: Leo Catozzo, with Assistant Editor Lina Caterini
ASSISTANT DIRECTOR: Moraldo Rossi
PRODUCERS: Dino De Laurentiis and Carlo Ponti
EXECUTIVE PRODUCERS: Danilo Fallani, Giorgio Morra, Angelo Cittadini
DIRECTOR OF PRODUCTION: Luigi Giacosi
PRODUCTION: Produzione Ponti-De Laurentiis
PREMIERE: Venice International Film Festival, 11 September 1954
PRIZES: Silver Lion at Venice Film Festival / Italian Film Critics' Award for Best Film and Best Director / New York Film Critics' Award for Best Director / Oscar for Best Foreign Film
FORMAT: 35mm, black & white
APPROXIMATE RUNNING TIME: 94'
LEAD ACTORS:

Gelsomina › Giulietta Masina
Zampanò › Anthony Quinn
Il Matto (The Fool) › Richard Basehart
Giraffa (circus owner) › Aldo Silvani
The widow › Marcella Rovere
The nun › Livia Venturini

1955
Il bidone (The Swindle)
STORY: Federico Fellini, Ennio Flaiano, Tullio Pinelli, from a Fellini idea
SCRIPT: Federico Fellini, Ennio Flaiano, Tullio Pinelli
ARTISTIC ADVISOR: Brunello Rondi
DIRECTOR OF PHOTOGRAPHY: Otello Martelli
CAMERAMAN: Roberto Gerardi with Assistant Cameraman Arturo Zavattini
SET DESIGN AND COSTUMES: Dario Cecchi
SOUND: Giovanni Rossi
MUSIC: Nino Rota
EDITING: Mario Serandrei and Giuseppe Vari
ASSISTANT DIRECTORS: Moraldo Rossi, Narciso Vicario, Dominique Delouche, Paolo Nuzzi
DIRECTOR OF PRODUCTION: Giuseppe Colizzi
PRODUCTION SECRETARY: Manolo Bolognini
PRODUCTION: Titanus (Rome) / SGC (Paris)
PREMIERE: Venice International Film Festival, 10 September 1955
FORMAT: 35mm, black & white
APPROXIMATE RUNNING TIME: 105'
LEAD ACTORS:

Augusto Rocca › Broderick Crawford
Roberto › Franco Fabrizi
Picasso › Richard Basehart
Iris › Giulietta Masina
Anna (crippled girl) › Sue Ellen Blake
Giacomo Gabrielli › Vargas

1957
Le notti di Cabiria (The Nights of Cabiria)
STORY: Federico Fellini, Ennio Flaiano, Tullio Pinelli, from a Fellini idea
SCRIPT: Federico Fellini, Ennio Flaiano, Tullio Pinelli, with collaboration of Pier Paolo Pasolini for dialogue
SCRIPT CONSULTANT: Brunello Rondi
PHOTOGRAPHY: Aldo Tonti, Otello Martelli

SET DESIGN AND COSTUMES: Piero Gherardi
SOUND: Roy Mangano
MUSIC: Nino Rota
EDITING: Leo Catozzo
ASSISTANT DIRECTORS: Moraldo Rossi and Dominique Delouche
PRODUCER: Dino De Laurentiis
DIRECTOR OF PRODUCTION: Luigi De Laurentiis
PRODUCTION SECRETARY: Narciso Vicario
PRODUCTION: Dino De Laurentiis (Rome) / Les Films Marceau (Paris)
PREMIERE: Cannes International Film Festival, 6 September 1957
PRIZES: Palme d'Or for Best Actress (Giulietta Masina)
FORMAT: 35mm, black & white
APPROXIMATE RUNNING TIME: 110'
LEAD ACTORS:

Cabiria Ceccarelli › Giulietta Masina
Oscar D'Onofrio › François Périer
Alberto Lazzari (movie star) › Amedeo Nazzari
Jessy (Lazzari's girlfriend) › Dorian Gray
Wanda (Cabiria's friend) › Franca Marzi
The magician › Aldo Silvani
The cripple › Mario Passange
Giorgio › Franco Fabrizi

1959
La dolce vita (La Dolce Vita)
STORY: Federico Fellini, Ennio Flaiano, Tullio Pinelli
SCRIPT: Federico Fellini, Ennio Flaiano, Tullio Pinelli, and Brunello Rondi
PHOTOGRAPHY: Otello Martelli
CAMERAMAN: Arturo Zavattini, with Assistant Ennio Guarnieri
SET DESIGN AND COSTUMES: Piero Gherardi
SOUND: Agostino Moretti, Oscar Di Santo
MAKEUP: Otello Fava
MUSIC: Nino Rota
EDITING: Leo Catozzo
ASSISTANT DIRECTORS: Guidarino Guidi, Paolo Nuzzi, Dominique Delouche
DIRECTOR'S ASSISTANTS: Gianfranco Mingozzi, Giancarlo Romani, Lilli Veenman
PRODUCERS: Angelo Rizzoli and Giuseppe Amato
EXECUTIVE PRODUCER: Franco Magli
DIRECTORS OF PRODUCTION: Manlio M. Moretti, Nello Meniconi
PRODUCTION SECRETARIES: Mario Basile, Mario De Biase, Osvaldo De Micheli
PRODUCTION: Riama Film (Rizzoli-Amato, Rome) / Pathé Consortium Cinéma (Paris)
PREMIERE: Milan, 5 February 1960
PRIZES: Italian Film Critics' Award for Best Idea, Best Lead Role, and Best Set Design / Palme d'Or at Cannes International Film Festival / Oscar for Best Costumes
FORMAT: 35mm, black & white / CinemaScope
APPROXIMATE RUNNING TIME: 178'
LEAD ACTORS:

Marcello Rubini › Marcello Mastroianni
Sylvia › Anita Ekberg
Maddalena › Anouk Aimée
Emma › Yvonne Furneaux
Steiner › Alan Cuny
Paparazzo › Walter Santesso
Robert › Lex Barker
Marcello's father › Annibale Ninchi
Fanny › Magali Noël
Laura › Laura Betti
Nadia › Nadia Gray

Paola › Valeria Ciangottini
Rock singer › Adriano Celentano
Girl in Via Veneto › Nico Otzak
Frankie Stout › Alan Dijon
Clown › Polidor

1962

Le tentazioni del dottor Antonio (The Temptations of Doctor Antonio), second episode in *Boccaccio '70 (Boccaccio '70)*, conceived by Cesare Zavattini

STORY: Federico Fellini

SCRIPT: Federico Fellini, Tullio Pinelli, Ennio Flaiano, with Brunello Rondo and Goffredo Parise

PHOTOGRAPHY: Otello Martelli

SET DESIGN: Piero Zuffi

MUSIC: Nino Rota

EDITING: Leo Catozzo

PRODUCERS: Carlo Ponti and Antonio Cervi

PRODUCTION: Concordia Compagnia Cinematografica and Cineriz (Rome) / Francinex and Gray Films (Paris)

PREMIERE: Milan, 22 February 1962

FORMAT: 35mm, Technicolor / CinemaScope

APPROXIMATE RUNNING TIME: 54'

LEAD ACTORS:

Dr. Antonio Mazzuolo › Peppino De Felippo
Anita › Anita Ekberg
Mazzuolo's sister › Donatella Della Nora
Commendatore La Pappa › Antonio Acqua
Cupid › Elenora Nagy

1963

8 ½ (8 ½)

STORY: Federico Fellini and Ennio Flaiano, from a Fellini idea

SCRIPT: Federico Fellini, Tullio Pinelli, Ennio Flaiano, Brunello Rondi

PHOTOGRAPHY: Gianni Di Venanzo

CAMERAMAN: Pasquale De Santis

SET DESIGN AND COSTUMES: Piero Gherardi

MAKEUP: Otello Fava

MUSIC: Nino Rota

EDITING: Leo Catozzo, with Assistant Editor Adriana Olasio

ASSISTANT DIRECTORS: Guidarino Guidi, Giulio Paradisi, Francesco Aluigi

PRODUCER: Angelo Rizzoli

EXECUTIVE PRODUCERS: Clemente Fracassi, Alessandro von Norman

DIRECTOR OF PRODUCTION: Nello Meniconi

PRODUCTION SECRETARY: Albino Morandin

PRODUCTION: Cineriz (Rome) / Francinex (Paris)

PREMIERE: Milan, 17 February 1963

PRIZES: Grand Prize, Moscow International Film Festival / Italian Film Critics' Award for Best Director, Best Producer, Best Subject, Best Screenplay, Best Music, Best Photography, and Best Female Second Role / New York Film Critics' Award / Two Oscars for Best Foreign Film and Best Costumes

FORMAT: 35mm, black & white / CinemaScope

APPROXIMATE RUNNING TIME: 141'

LEAD ACTORS:

Guido Anselmi › Marcello Mastroianni
Luisa (Guido's wife) › Anouk Aimée
Carla (Guido's mistress) › Sandra Milo
La Saraghina › Edra Gale
Claudia (actress) › Claudia Cardinale
Rossella › Rossella Falk

Gloria › Barbara Steel
Pace (the producer) › Guido Alberti
Mezzabotta › Mario Pisu
French actress › Madeleine Lebeau
Daumier (the critic) › Jean Rougeul
Beautiful mystery woman › Caterina Boratto
Maurice the Magician › Ian Dallas
The Cardinal › Tito Masini
Guido's father › Annibale Ninchi
Guido's mother › Giuditta Rissone
Guido (as a schoolboy) › Marco Gemini
Jacqueline Bonbon › Yvonne Cassadei

1965

Giulietta degli spiriti (Juliet of the Spirits)

STORY: Federico Fellini and Tullio Pinelli, from a Fellini idea

SCRIPT: Federico Fellini, Tullio Pinelli, Ennio Flaiano, and Brunello Rondi

DIRECTOR OF PHOTOGRAPHY: Gianni Di Venanzo

CAMERAMAN: Pasquale De Santis

SET DESIGN AND COSTUMES: Piero Gherardi

MAKEUP: Otello Fava and Eligio Trani

MUSIC: Nino Rota

SOUND: Mario Faraoni, Mario Morici

EDITING: Ruggero Mastroianni

ASSISTANT DIRECTORS: Francesco Aluigi, Liliana Betti, Rosalba Zavoli

PRODUCER: Angelo Rizzoli

EXECUTIVE PRODUCER: Clemente Fracassi

DIRECTORS OF PRODUCTION: Mario Basili, Alessandro von Norman

PRODUCTION SECRETARIES: Renato Fié, Ennio Onorati

PRODUCTION: Federiz (Rome) / Francoriz (Paris)

PREMIERE: Rome, 22 October 1965

FORMAT: 35mm, Technicolor / CinemaScope

APPROXIMATE RUNNING TIME: 129'

LEAD ACTORS:

Giulietta › Giulietta Masina
Giorgio › Mario Pisu
Susy/Iris/Fanny › Sandra Milo
Giulietta's mother › Caterina Boratto
The grandfather › Lou Gilbert
Bhisma › Valeska Gert
Detective Lynx-Eyes › Alberto Plebani
Dolores (Dolly) › Silvana Jachino
Val › Valentina Cortesa
José › José Luis de Villalonga
Arabian Prince › Fred Williams

1968

Toby Dammit (Toby Dammit), third episode in *Tre passi nel delirio (Spirits of the Dead)*

STORY: Edgar Allan Poe, a free adaptation of his short story, "Never Bet the Devil Your Head"

SCRIPT: Federico Fellini and Bernardino Zapponi

DIRECTOR OF PHOTOGRAPHY: Giuseppe Rotunno

SET DESIGN, MAKEUP, AND COSTUMES: Piero Tosi, based on Fellini's concepts

SPECIAL EFFECTS: Joseph Nathanson

MUSIC: Nino Rota

EDITING: Ruggero Mastroianni

ASSISTANT DIRECTORS: Eschilo Tarquini, Francesco Aluigi, Liliana Betti

PRODUCER: Alberto Grimaldi

EXECUTIVE PRODUCER: Enzo Provenzale

DIRECTOR OF PRODUCTION: Tommaso Sagone

PRODUCTION: PEA (Rome) / Les Films Marceau (Paris) / Cocinor (Paris)
PREMIERE: Cannes International Film Festival, 17 May 1968
FORMAT: 35mm, Eastmancolor / CinemaScope
APPROXIMATE RUNNING TIME: 37'
LEAD ACTORS:
Toby Dammit › Terence Stamp
Father Spagna › Salvo Randone
The Actress › Antonia Pietrosi
The Devil Girl › Marina Yaru

1968
Block-notes di un regista (Fellini: A Director's Notebook)
STORY: Federico Fellini and Bernardino Zapponi
SCRIPT: Federico Fellini and Bernardino Zapponi, with English dialogue by Eugene Walter
DIRECTOR OF PHOTOGRAPHY: Pasquale De Santis
SET DESIGN AND COSTUMES: Federico Fellini
MUSIC: Nino Rota
EDITING: Ruggero Mastroianni, with Assistant Editor Adriana Olasio
ASSISTANT DIRECTORS: Maurizio Mein, Liliana Betti
PRODUCER: Peter Goldfarb
EXECUTIVE PRODUCER: Lamberto Pippia
PRODUCTION: NBC Productions International (USA)
PREMIERE: NBC, 11 April 1969
FORMAT: 16mm, Eastmancolor / Normal
APPROXIMATE RUNNING TIME: 60'
LEAD ACTORS (AS THEMSELVES):
Fellini
Giulietta Masina
Marcello Mastroianni
Caterina Boratto
Genius the Medium

1969
Fellini Satyricon (Fellini's Satyricon)
STORY: Petronius Arbiter, a freely adapted version of his *Satyricon*
SCRIPT: Federico Fellini and Bernardino Zapponi, with collaboration of Brunello Rondi
DIRECTOR OF PHOTOGRAPHY: Giuseppe Rotunno
CAMERAMAN: Giuseppe Maccari
SET DESIGN AND COSTUMES: Danilo Donati, based on Fellini's concepts
MAKEUP: Piero Tosi and Rino Carboni
SPECIAL EFFECTS: Adriano Pischiutta
MUSIC: Nino Rota, Ilhan Mimaroglu, Tod Dockstader, and Andrew Rudin
SOUND: Oscar De Arcangelis
EDITING: Ruggero Mastroianni, with Assistant Editor Adriana Olasio
ASSISTANT DIRECTOR: Maurizio Mein
PRODUCER: Alberto Grimaldi
EXECUTIVE PRODUCER: Enzo Provenzale
DIRECTOR OF PRODUCTION: Roberto Cocco
PRODUCTION SECRETARY: Michele Pesce
PRODUCTION: PEA (Rome) / Les Artistes Associés (Paris)
PREMIERE: Venice International Film Festival, 4 September 1969
FORMAT: 35mm, Technicolor / Panavision
APPROXIMATE RUNNING TIME: 138'
LEAD ACTORS:
Encolpio › Martin Potter
Ascilto › Hiram Keller
Gitone › Max Born

Trimalchione › Mario Romagnoli
Eumolpo › Salvo Randone
Vernacchio › Fanfulla
Fortunata › Magali Noël
Lica › Alain Cuny
Trifena › Capucine
Slave girl › Hylette Adolphe
Husband suicide › Joseph Wheeler
Oenothea › Donyale Luna
Nymphomaniac › Sibilla Sedat
Hermaphrodite › Pasquale Baldassare

1970
I clowns (The Clowns)
STORY AND SCRIPT: Federico Fellini and Bernardino Zapponi
DIRECTOR OF PHOTOGRAPHY: Dario Di Palma
CAMERAMAN: Blasco Giurato
SET DESIGN AND COSTUMES: Danilo Donati, based on Fellini's concepts
MAKEUP: Rino Carboni
MUSIC: Nino Rota
SOUND: Alberto Bartolomei
EDITING: Ruggero Mastroianni, with Assistant Editor Adriana Olasio
ASSISTANT DIRECTORS: Maurizio Mein and Liliana Betti
PRODUCERS: Elio Scardamaglia, Ugo Guerra
DIRECTOR OF PRODUCTION: Lamberto Pippia
PRODUCTION: RAI (Rome) / ORTF (Paris) / Bavaria Film (Munich) / Compagnia Leone Cinematografica (Rome)
PREMIERE: RAI TV, 25 December 1970
FORMAT: 35mm, Technicolor
APPROXIMATE RUNNING TIME: 90'
LEAD ACTORS:
(Fellini's troupe)
The Director › Fellini
Script girl › Maya Morin
Cameraman › Gasperino
Soundman › Alvaro Vitali
Assistant › Lina Alberti
(as themselves)
Anita Ekberg
Pierre Etaix
Annie and Victor Fratellini
Victoria Chaplin
Tristan Rémy
(Italian clowns)
Billi, Scotti, Fanfulla, Rizzo, Pistoni, Furia, Sbarra, Carini, Terzo
(French clowns)
Alex, Père Loriot, Maiss, Bario, Ludo, Charlie Rivel, Nino

1972
Roma (Fellini's Roma)
STORY AND SCRIPT: Federico Fellini and Bernardino Zapponi
DIRECTOR OF PHOTOGRAPHY: Giuseppe Rotunno
CAMERAMAN: Giuseppe Maccari
SET DESIGN AND COSTUMES: Danilo Donati, based on Fellini's concepts
MAKEUP: Rino Carboni
FRESCOES AND PORTRAITS: Rinaldo, Antonello, and Giuliano Geleng, based on Fellini's concepts
SPECIAL EFFECTS: Adriano Pischiutta
MUSIC: Nino Rota
SOUND: Renato Cadueri
EDITING: Ruggero Mastroianni, with Assistant Editors Adriana Olasio and Leda Bellini
ASSISTANT DIRECTOR: Maurizio Mein, Paolo Pietrangeli, Tonino Antonucci

PRODUCER: Turi Vasile

EXECUTIVE PRODUCER: Danilo Marciani

DIRECTOR OF PRODUCTION: Lamberto Pippia

PRODUCTION: Ultra Film (Rome) / Les Artistes Associés (Paris)

PREMIERE: Cannes International Film Festival, 14 March 1972

FORMAT: 35mm, Technicolor / CinemaScope

APPROXIMATE RUNNING TIME: 128'

LEAD ACTORS:

Fellini > Himself

Young Fellini > Peter Gonzales

Dolores (prostitute) > Fiora Florence

The Princess > Pia De Doses

The Cardinal > Renato Giovannoli

(cameos)

Gore Vidal

John Francis Lane

Anna Magnani

1973

Amarcord (Amarcord)

STORY AND SCRIPT: Federico Fellini and Tonino Guerra, from a Fellini idea

DIRECTOR OF PHOTOGRAPHY: Giuseppe Rotunno

CAMERAMAN: Giuseppe Maccari

SET DESIGN AND COSTUMES: Danilo Donati, based on Fellini's concepts

MAKEUP: Rino Carboni

SPECIAL EFFECTS: Adriano Pischiutta

MUSIC: Nino Rota

SOUND: Oscar De Arcangelis

DUBBING: Mario Maldessi

EDITING: Ruggero Mastroianni, with Assistant Editor Adriana Olasio

ASSISTANT DIRECTOR: Maurizio Mein, Liliana Betti, Gerald Morin, Mario Garriba

PRODUCER: Franco Cristaldi

DIRECTOR OF PRODUCTION: Lamberto Pippia

PRODUCTION SECRETARIES: Fernando Rossi, Giuseppe Bruno Bossio

PRODUCTION: FC Produzione (Rome) / PECF (Paris)

PREMIERE: (in Italy), 18 December 1973

PRIZES: Italian Film Critics' Award / New York Film Critics' Award / Oscar for Best Foreign Film

FORMAT: 35mm, Technicolor / CinemaScope

APPROXIMATE RUNNING TIME: 123'

LEAD ACTORS:

Titta > Bruno Zanin

Titta's mother > Pupella Maggio

Titta's father > Armando Brancia

Titta's grandfather > Peppino Ianigro

Uncle Teo > Ciccio Ingrassia

La Gradisca > Magali Noël

Biscein the liar > Gennaro Ombra

The lawyer > Luigi Rossi

Buxom tobacconist > Maria Beluzzi

Volpina > Josiane Tanzilli

Fascist Leader > Ferrucio Brembilla

Headmaster Zeus > Franco Magno

1976

Casanova (Fellini's Casanova)

STORY: Giacomo Casanova, freely based on his *Story of My Life*

SCRIPT: Federico Fellini and Bernadino Zapponi, poetry by Andrea Zanzotto

CONSULTANTS: Gore Vidal, Anthony Burgess

DIRECTOR OF PHOTOGRAPHY: Giuseppe Rotunno

CAMERAMAN: Massimo Di Venanzo

SET DESIGN AND COSTUMES: Danilo Donati, based on Fellini's concepts

MAKEUP: Rino Carboni, Gianetto De Rossi

HAIRDRESSER: Vitaliana Patacca

MUSIC: Nino Rota

SOUND: Oscar De Arcangelis

EDITING: Ruggero Mastroianni, with Assistant Editors Adriana and Marcello Olasio

ASSISTANT DIRECTORS: Maurizio Mein, Liliana Betti, Gerald Morin

PRODUCER: Alberto Grimaldi (with Daniel Toscan du Plantier)

EXECUTIVE PRODUCER: Giorgio Morra

DIRECTOR OF PRODUCTION: Lamberto Pippia

PRODUCTION SECRETARIES: Titti Pesaro, Luciano Bonomi

PRODUCTION: PEA (Rome)

PREMIERE: (in Italy), 11 December 1976

PRIZE: Oscar for Best Costumes

FORMAT: 35mm, Technicolor / CinemaScope

APPROXIMATE RUNNING TIME: 170' (Italian version)

LEAD ACTORS:

Casanova > Donald Sutherland

Madame d'Urfé > Cicely Browne

Enrichetta > Tina Aumont

Sister Maddalena > Margareth Clementi

Isabella > Olimpia Carlisi

Astrodi > Marika Rivera

Barberina > Chesty Morgan

Saint Germain > Harold Innocent

Dubois > Daniel Emilfork

Giantess > Sandy Allen

The Charpillons > Carmen Scarpitta and Diane Kurys

The "Doll" > Angela Lojodice

Wanton hunchback > Angelica Hansen

Duke of Würtemberg > Dudley Sutton

Dr. Moebius > Mario Cencelli

1978

Prova d'orchestra (Orchestra Rehearsal)

STORY: Federico Fellini

SCRIPT: Federico Fellini and Brunello Rondi

DIRECTOR OF PHOTOGRAPHY: Giuseppe Rotunno

CAMERAMAN: Gianni Fiore

SET DESIGN AND COSTUMES: Dante Ferretti and Gabriella Pescucci, based on Fellini's concepts

SPECIAL EFFECTS: Adriano Pischiutta

MUSIC: Nino Rota

SOUND: Carlo Baccarini

EDITING: Ruggero Mastroianni

ASSISTANT DIRECTOR: Maurizio Mein

PRODUCERS: Mimmo Scarano, Leo Pescarolo (with Daniel Toscan du Plantier)

EXECUTIVE PRODUCER: Lamberto Pippia

PRODUCTION: Daimo Cinematografica and RAI TV (Rome) / Albatros Produktion (Munich)

PREMIERE: Rome, 19 October 1978

FORMAT: 35mm, Technicolor

APPROXIMATE RUNNING TIME: 70'

LEAD ACTORS:

Orchestra conductor > Balduin Baas

First violinist > David Mauhsell

Copyist > Umberto Zuanelli

Violinists > Angelica Hansen and Heinz Kreuger

Harpist > Clara Colosimo

Pianist > Elizabeth Labi
Cellist > Ferdinando Villella
Interviewer's voice > Fellini

1980

La città delle donne (City of Women)

STORY AND SCRIPT: Federico Fellini and Bernardino Zapponi with Brunello Rondi
DIRECTOR OF PHOTOGRAPHY: Giuseppe Rotunno
CAMERAMAN: Gianni Fiore
SET DESIGN AND COSTUMES: Dante Ferretti and Gabriella Pescucci, based on Fellini's concepts
MAKEUP: Rino Carboni
PAINTING AND FRESCOES: Rinaldo and Giuliano Geleng, based on Fellini's concepts
SCULPTURE: Giovanni Gianese
SPECIAL EFFECTS: Adriano Pischiutta
MUSIC: Luis Bacalov
SOUND AND MIXING: Tomaso Quattrini, Pierre Lorrain, and Fausto Ancillai
EDITING: Ruggero Mastroianni, with Assistant Editors Adriana Olasio, Bruno Sarandrea, and Bruno Puglisi
ASSISTANT DIRECTORS: Maurizio Mein and Jean-Louis Godfrey (2nd Unit)
CASTING: Liliana Betti
PRODUCER: Daniel Toscan du Plantier (with Franco Rossellini)
EXECUTIVE PRODUCER: Lamberto Pippia
DIRECTORS OF PRODUCTION: Francesco Orefici, Philippe Lorain Bernard
PRODUCTION: Opera Film Produzione (Rome) / Gaumont (Paris)
PREMIERE: Cannes International Film Festival, 19 May 1980
FORMAT: 35mm, Technicolor / CinemaScope
APPROXIMATE RUNNING TIME: 140'
LEAD ACTORS:
Snàporaz > Marcello Mastroianni
His wife > Anna Prucnal
Mystery woman on train > Bernice Stegers
Katzone > Ettore Manni
Katzone's 10.000th mistress > Carla Terlizzi
The two soubrettes > Donatella Damiani and Rosaria Tafuri

1983

E la nave va (And the Ship Sails On)

STORY AND SCRIPT: Federico Fellini and Tonino Guerra, with opera lyrics by Andrea Zanzotto
DIRECTOR OF PHOTOGRAPHY: Giuseppe Rotunno
SET DESIGN AND COSTUMES: Dante Ferretti and Maurizio Millenotti, based on Fellini's concepts
SPECIAL EFFECTS: Adriano Pischiutta
MUSIC: Gianfranco Plenizio
SOUND: Riccardo Cucciolla
FRENCH DUBBING: Bertrand Philbert
EDITING: Ruggero Mastroianni
ASSISTANT DIRECTOR: Giovanni Arduini, Andrea De Carlo
PRODUCERS: Franco Cristaldi (with Daniel Toscan du Plantier)
ASSOCIATE PRODUCER: Aldo Nemni
EXECUTIVE PRODUCER: Pietro Notarianni
DIRECTOR OF PRODUCTION: Lucio Orlandini
PRODUCTION: RAI / Vides Produzione (Rome) / Gaumont (Paris)
PREMIERE: Venice International Film Festival, 10 September 1983
FORMAT: 35mm, Technicolor / CinemaScope
APPROXIMATE RUNNING TIME: 132'

LEAD ACTORS:
Orlando > Freddie Jones
Ildebranda Cuffari > Barbara Jefford
Edmea Tetua > Janet Suzman
Princess Lherimia > Pina Bausch
Aureliano Fuciletto > Victor Poletti
Sir Reginald Dongby > Peter Cellier
Lady Dongby > Norma West
Grand Duke of Herzog > Fiorenzo Serra
Count of Bassano > Pasquale Zito

1985

Ginger e Fred (Ginger and Fred)

STORY: Federico Fellini and Tonino Guerra
SCRIPT: Federico Fellini, Tonino Guerra, and Tullio Pinelli
DIRECTOR OF PHOTOGRAPHY: Tonino Delli Colli and Ennio Guarnieri
SET DESIGN AND COSTUMES: Dante Ferretti and Danilo Donati, based on Fellini's concepts
CHOREOGRAPHY: Tony Ventura
SPECIAL EFFECTS: Adriano Pischiutta
MUSIC: Nicola Piovani
SOUND: Sergio Marcotulli
EDITING: Nino Baragli, Ugo De Rossi, Ruggero Mastroianni
ASSISTANT DIRECTOR: Gianni Arduini
DIRECTOR'S ASSISTANTS: Filippo Ascione, Daniela Barbiani, Eugenio Cappuccio, Anke Zindler
PRODUCER: Alberto Grimaldi
EXECUTIVE PRODUCER: Luigi Millozza
DIRECTORS OF PRODUCTION: Walter Massi, Gianfranco Coduti, Roberto Mannoni, Raymond Leplont
PRODUCTION: RAI-UNO and PEA (Rome) / REVCOM Films, Les Films Ariane, FR3 Films (Paris) / Stella Film (Monaco)
PREMIERE: Rome, 13 January 1986
FORMAT: 35mm, color
APPROXIMATE RUNNING TIME: 125'
LEAD ACTORS:
Amelia ("Ginger") > Giulietta Masina
Pippo ("Fred") > Marcello Mastroianni
TV host > Franco Fabrizi
The Admiral > Frederick Ledenburg
The Flying Friar > Jacques Henri Lartigue
The Transvestite > Augusto Poderosi
"Clark Gable" > Salvatore Billa
"Woody Allen" > Fabrizio Libralesco
"Marcel Proust" > Leonardo Petrillo
"Franz Kafka" > Renato Grilli
"Marty Feldman" > Daniele Aldovrandi
"Marlene Dietrich" > Barbara Golinska
"Kojak" > Eolo Capritti
"Ronald Reagan" > Carlo di Placido

1987

Intervista (Interview)

STORY: Federico Fellini
SCRIPT: Federico Fellini, with collaboration of Gianfranco Angelucci
DIRECTOR OF PHOTOGRAPHY: Tonino Delli Colli
SET DESIGN AND COSTUMES: Danilo Donati, based on Fellini's concepts
MUSIC: Nicola Piovani, with additional music by Nino Rota from past Fellini films
SOUND AND MIXING: Luciano and Massimo Anzellotti, Sergio Marcotulli

DOLBY: Romano Pampaloni and Federico Savina
EDITING: Nino Baragli
ASSISTANT DIRECTOR: Maurizio Mein
PRODUCER: Ibrahim Moussa
EXECUTIVE PRODUCER: Pietro Notarianni
ASSOCIATE PRODUCER: FERNLYN
PRODUCTION SUPERVISOR: Michele Janczarek
PRODUCTION: Aljosha Productions, RAI-UNO and Cinecittà (Rome)
PREMIERE: Cannes International Film Festival, 18 May 1987
PRIZES: Grand Prize, 15th Moscow International Film Festival / Special Prize for the 40th Cannes Festival Anniversary / AGIS-BNL Prize
FORMAT: 35mm, color
APPROXIMATE RUNNING TIME: 112′
LEAD ACTORS:
Young journalist › Sergio Rubini
Saxophone player › Antonella Ponziani
Matinée idol › Paola Liguori
Cinecittà custodian › Nadia Ottaviani
(as themselves)
Federico Fellini
Anita Ekberg
Marcello Mastroianni (and as Mandrake the Magician)
Maurizio Mein

1990

La voce della luna (The Voice of the Moon)
STORY: Ermanno Cavazzoni, freely adapted from his novel *Il poema dei lunatici*
SCRIPT: Federico Fellini, in collaboration with Tullio Pinelli and Ermanno Cavazzoni
DIRECTOR OF PHOTOGRAPHY: Tonino Delli Colli
CAMERAMAN: Marco Sperduti
SET DESIGN AND COSTUMES: Dante Ferretti and Maurizio Millenotti
MUSICAL COMMENTARY: Nicola Piovani
SOUND: Tommasso Quatrini
EDITING: Nino Baragli
PRODUCERS: Mario and Vittorio Cecchi Gori
EXECUTIVE PRODUCERS: Bruno Altissimi and Claudio Saraceni
PRODUCTION: C.G. Group Tiger Cinematografica and RAI-Uno (Rome) / Films A2, La SEPT and Cinemax (Paris)
FORMAT: 35mm, color
PREMIERE: (in Italy), 31 January 1990
APPROXIMATE RUNNING TIME: 120′
LEAD ACTORS:
Ivo Salvini › Roberto Benigni
Prefect Gonnella › Paolo Villaggio
Marisa ("the steam train") › Marisa Tomasi
Nestore › Angelo Orlando
Oboe player › Sim
Aldina Ferruzzi › Nadia Ottaviani
Ivo's grandmother › Uta Schmidt

Television Commercials Directed by Fellini

1984

Campari Soda television commercial
TITLE: *Oh, che bel paesaggio!*
Barilla pasta television commercial

1992

Three Banca di Roma television commercials of 90 seconds each
LEAD ACTORS: Paolo Villaggio, Fernando Rey, Anna Falchi

Films Scripted for Other Directors

1939

Imputato alzatevi! (Defendant, On Your Feet!)
DIRECTOR: Mario Mattoli
SCRIPT: Vittorio Metz, Mario Mattoli (Fellini not credited)

Lo vedi come sei? (Do You See How You Are?)
DIRECTOR: Mario Mattoli
SCRIPT: Vittorio Metz, Steno, Mario Mattoli (Fellini not credited)

1940

Non me lo dire! (Don't Tell Me!)
DIRECTOR: Mario Mattoli
SCRIPT: Vittorio Metz, Marcello Marchesi, Steno, Mario Mattoli (Fellini not credited)

I pirata sono io (The Pirate Is Me)
DIRECTOR: Mario Mattoli
SCRIPT: Vittorio Metz, Steno, Marcello Marchesi, Mario Mattoli (Fellini not credited)

1942

Avanti c'è posto (There's Room Up Ahead)
DIRECTOR: Mario Bonnard
SCRIPT: Aldo Fabrizi, Cesare Zavattini, Piero Tellini, Federico Fellini (credited as "Federico")

Documento Z3 (Document Z3)
DIRECTOR: Alfredo Guarini
SCRIPT: Sandro De Feo, Alfredo Guarini, Ercoli Patti (Fellini not credited)

1943

Campo de' fiori (Campo de' fiori Square)
DIRECTOR: Mario Bonnard
SCRIPT: Aldo Fabrizi, Federico Fellini, Piero Tellini, Mario Bonnard

L'ultima carrozzela (The Last Carriage)
DIRECTOR: Mario Mattoli
SCRIPT: Aldo Fabrizi, Federico Fellini

Quarta pagina (The Fourth Page)
DIRECTOR: Nicola Manzari, Domenico Gambino
SCRIPT (SEVEN EPISODES SCRIPTED BY DIFFERENT WRITERS): Piero Tellini, Federico Fellini, Edoardo Anton, Ugo Betti, Nicola Manzari, Spiro Manzari, Giuseppe Marotta, Gianni Puccini, Steno, Cesare Zavattini

Chi l'ha visto? (Who Has Seen Him?)
DIRECTOR: Goffredo Alessandrini
SCRIPT: Federico Fellini, Piero Tellini

Gli ultimi Tuareg (The Last Tuaregs)
DIRECTORS: Gino Talamo, Osvaldo Valenti (with Fellini possibly directing a few scenes)
SCRIPT: Federico Fellini, Tito Silvio Mursino (alias Vittorio Mussolini), Osvaldo Valenti

1944

Apparizione (Apparition)
DIRECTOR: Jean de Limur
SCRIPT: Piero Tellini, Lucio De Caro, Giuseppe Amato (Fellini not credited)

Tutta la città canta (The Whole City Is Singing)
DIRECTOR: Riccardo Freda
SCRIPT: Vittorio Metz, Marcello Marchesi, Steno (Fellini not credited)

1945

Roma città aperta (Rome, Open City)
DIRECTOR: Roberto Rossellini
SCRIPT: Alberto Consiglio, Sergio Amidei, Roberto Rosellini, Federico Fellini (also served as Rossellini's assistant)

1946

Paisà (Paisan)
DIRECTOR: Roberto Rossellini
SCRIPT: Sergio Amidei, Klaus Mann, Alfred Hayes, Marcello Pagliero, Roberto Rossellini, Federico Fellini

1947

Il delitto di Giovanni Episcopo (The Crime of Giovanni Episcopo)
DIRECTOR: Alberto Lattuada
SCRIPT: Piero Tellini, Suso Cecchi D'Amico, Aldo Fabrizi, Alberto Lattuada, Federico Fellini

Il passatore (A Bullet for Stefano)
DIRECTOR: Duilio Coletti
SCRIPT: Cesare Zavattini, Tullio Pinelli, Federico Fellini, Duilio Coletti

1948

Senza pietà (Without Pity)
DIRECTOR: Alberto Lattuada
SCRIPT: Tullio Pinelli, Alberto Lattuada, Federico Fellini (also Assistant Director), Ettore Maria Margadonna. *Note:* Giulietta Masina's first film appearance

Il miracolo (The Miracle), Part 2 of *L'amore (The Ways of Love)*
DIRECTOR: Roberto Rossellini
SCRIPT: Federico Fellini (also stars as a stranger who seduces a peasant girl played by Anna Magnani), Tullio Pinelli, Roberto Rossellini

1949

Il mulino del Po (The Mill on the Po)
DIRECTOR: Alberto Lattuada
SCRIPT: Ricardo Bacchelli, Mario Bonfantini, Luigi Comencini, Carlo Musso, Sergio Romano, Alberto Lattuada, Tullio Pinelli, Federico Fellini

In nome della legge (In the Name of the Law)
DIRECTOR: Pietro Germi
SCRIPT: Aldo Bizzari, Pietro Germi, Giuseppe Mangione, Mario Monicelli, Tullio Pinelli, Federico Fellini

1950

Francesco, giullare di Dio (The Flowers of Saint Francis)
DIRECTOR: Roberto Rossellini
SCRIPT: Roberto Rossellini and Federico Fellini (also Assistant Director), with Father Antonio Lisandrini and Father Félix Morlion as script consultants

Il cammino della speranza (The Path of Hope)
DIRECTOR: Pietro Germi
SCRIPT: Pietro Germi, Tullio Pinelli, Federico Fellini

1951

La città si difende (The City Defends Itself)
DIRECTOR: Pietro Germi
SCRIPT: Pietro Germi, Tullio Pinelli, Giuseppe Mangione, Federico Fellini

Persiana chiuse (Drawn Shutters)
DIRECTOR: Luigi Comencini
SCRIPT: Tullio Pinelli, Federico Fellini

1952

Europa '51 (Europe '51)
DIRECTOR: Roberto Rossellini
SCRIPT: Sandro De Feo, Roberto Rossellini, Mario Pannunzio, Ivo Perilli, Diego Fabbri, Antonio Pietrangeli, Brunello Rondi (Fellini not credited; worked on treatment only)

Il brigante di Tacca del Lupo (The Bandit of Tacca del Lupo)
DIRECTOR: Pietro Germi
SCRIPT: Tullio Pinelli, Pietro Germi, Fausto Tozzi, Federico Fellini

Fortunella (Fortunella)
DIRECTOR: Eduardo De Filippo
SCRIPT: Federico Fellini

Viaggio con Anita (A Journey with Anita)
DIRECTOR: Mario Monicelli
SCRIPT: Tullio Pinelli (Fellini not credited at his request)

Filmography compiled by Damian Pettigrew from the credits of all of Fellini's films, with additional material verified from a multitude of sources, including *Sight and Sound*, *Cahiers du cinéma*, *Positif*, *Etudes cinématographiques*, *L'Arc*, *Cinématographe*, *L'Avant scène cinéma*, *Fellini* by Gilbert Salachas, *The Cinema of Federico Fellini* by Peter Bondanella, *Fellini: A Life* by Hollis Alpert, *Fellini on Fellini* by Costanzo Costantini, *Federico Fellini* by Lietta Tornabuoni, and *Fellini* by Tullio Kezich.

Acknowledgments

I could never have completed my work without the friendship and counsel of Olivier Gal, Gilbert Finetin, Gian Luca Farinelli, Tullio Pinelli, Fernanda and Iole Bellagamba, Tullio Kezich, Daniel Denis, and at ARTE France Thierry Garrel, Delphine Coulin, and Pierrette Ominetti. For their support I am deeply grateful.

EDITOR: Deborah Aaronson
DESIGNER: Brankica Kovrlija
PRODUCTION MANAGER: Jane Searle

LIBRARY OF CONGRESS CATALOGING-IN-PUBLICATION DATA

Fellini, Federico.
 I'm a born liar : a Fellini lexicon / edited by Damian Pettigrew.
   p. cm.
Filmography: p.
Includes bibliographical references and index.
 ISBN 0-8109-4617-3
 1. Fellini, Federico—Interviews. 2. Motion picture producers and directors—Italy—Interviews. I. Pettigrew, Damian. II. Title.

 PN1998.3.F45A5 2003
 791.43'0233'092—dc21

                         2003011336

All text translated from the original italian by Damian Pettigrew.
Tullio Kezich's essay was translated by Samantha Topol and Damian Pettigrew.

"Truth and Poetry in Lies" copyright © 2003 Tullio Kezich
Copyright © 2003 Damian Pettigrew

Printed and bound in China

10 9 8 7 6 5 4 3 2 1

HARRY N. ABRAMS, INC.
100 Fifth Avenue
New York, N.Y. 10011
www.abramsbooks.com

Abrams is a subsidiary of

PAGES 4-5: Fellini framing night shots of cheering townspeople. (*Amarcord*, 1973)

PHOTOGRAPH CREDITS
Photograph research by Olivier Gal and Damian Pettigrew.

All photographs provided exclusively by and in collaboration with the Cineteca del Comune di Bologna except the following: Pages 60 and 86 courtesy Cinemazero. Copyright Gideon Bachmann. Pages 16, 30, 35, 40, 41, 43, 65, 82, 83, 90, 96, 97, 118, 124, 125, 137, 139, 144, 145, 146, 151, 157, and 161 courtesy collection of Les Archives du 7e Art. Pages 14, 15, 61, and 134 courtesy Portrait & Company. Copyright Iole Bellagamba. Pages 21 and 154-55 courtesy CHRISTOPHEL (Paris).

Cineteca Bologna